The Reflection of Life

The Practical Guide to Knowing Yourself Better and Excelling in Life

Nelson Cheng PhD (H. C.), SRF

To order additional copies of this book, contact
Toll Free +65 3165 7531 (Singapore)
Toll Free +60 3 3099 4412 (Malaysia)
www.partridgepublishing.com/singapore
orders.singapore@partridgepublishing.com

ISBN
ISBN: 978-1-5437-7170-1 (sc)
ISBN: 978-1-5437-7172-5 (hc)
ISBN: 978-1-5437-7171-8 (e)

Print information available on the last page.

12/13/2022

PARTRIDGE

PREFACE

What is the purpose of my existence?

What is my fundamental role on this earth?

Why did God put me on this earth?

I reflect often on these three questions as a Christian businessman and inventor. It is through constant reflection on these three questions that I discovered that one of the primary purposes of my existence is to solve problems through research and the development of new products to solve existential unsolved problems in the industry.

As I saw my little inventions contributing to the socio-economic progress of my staff and global distributors, my fundamental role on this earth became clear to me. Thus, my primary role on this earth is to contribute to the social and economic advancement of those who cross my path. It brought me deep satisfaction and contentment in my life to see former salespeople, engineers, managers, etc. ascend the socio-economic ladder no matter where they came from in the developed and developing world.

I found the answer to the question of 'Why did God put me on this earth?' after reading Matthew 5:16

> *Let your light so shine before men, that they may see your good works, and glorify your Father which is in heaven.*
> —Matthew 5:16

To do good work means to do anything that helps humanity or makes society a better place through my inventions.

The Reflection of Life is a book that has been written to motivate anyone reading it to fulfil their life purpose as they journey through this world. It is written to motivate those who may not criss-cross my path in life.

The Reflection of Life is a collection of my personal written quotations based on my life journey, experiences, and constant reflections of my life over the years.

Our thoughts and feelings are the difference between an intelligent robot and us. It is these feelings that make people human. It is our thoughts and feelings that set us apart from an intelligent robot. We are human because of these feelings.
—Nelson Cheng

From now on, brothers and sisters, if anything is excellent and if anything is admirable, focus your thoughts on these things: all that is true, all that is holy, all that is just, all that is pure, all that is lovely, and all that is worthy of praise.
—Philippians 4:8

FOREWORD

Having known Dr Nelson Cheng for more than 15 years, I have found him to be very passionate about all his endeavours, and always willing to share his knowledge and experiences with others.

He has condensed his experiences over the past 35 years into this forty-chapter book Reflection of Life.

We learn lessons from life on a continuous basis. This book directs us to pay attention to what we learn and acknowledge our goals to improve ourselves, by doing so, positively impact the people around us.

Reflecting on life's situations and experiences is something we should do consciously every now and then. Would things have been different if we had done them differently? Were there any lessons to be learned from these? Can we achieve a different outcome next time if we change something? All these questions are essential for the betterment of our lives.

There are roller coasters in life. Find and offer only what's good within us so we can turn it into genuine fun. Being a good person takes effort, as strange as it sounds. The process requires self-awareness. Perseverance is required. Although you may not fully understand everything that is different, you should keep an open mind about it.

Reflection of life is indeed a good book for anyone who is still struggling in life due to a lack of reflection on their life.

Highly recommended for all working adults, tertiary students, etc.

Prof Maria Amparo Oliveros Ruiz
Research Professor Faculty of Pedagogy
Autonomous University of Baja California

FOREWORD

The book highlights the importance of dedicating daily time to meditate about our lives. Nowadays this is relevant because we are living in a digital distraction era where everybody is competing to attract and gain our attention and if we are not careful our focus is easily lost causing some delays in the pursuit of our dreams and in the fulfillment of our destiny.

Dr. Nelson Cheng has a humble and noble heart. He is a living example of a visionary man, husband, family man, entrepreneur, inventor, businessman, innovator, and a man of God highly committed to adding value to society. He shares insights from his deep heart that will help you to thrive in life and shape your future. Success leaves its marks; hence, you can take advantage of it through his work.

This book is a creative, practical, and powerful tool to meditate and reflect on the perspectives, thoughts, and wisdom acquired by Dr. Cheng along his own successful and meaningful journey. He invites the reader to self-reflect on its own experiences, actions, thoughts, struggles, and failures, and learn from them to improve and grow. Also, it encourages us to think and live intentionally. It makes the call to be action-oriented people.

"Reflections of Life" is full of seeds of value and greatness. It is pure gold. I found it to be a source of wisdom. It is very helpful to unleash the potential of the current and new generations and empower them to develop a growth mindset and live meaningful lives. I see this work as a gift to humankind delivered by Dr. Cheng.

As a passionate about personal growth, I can tell you that this is a treasure that will provide great benefit to your life and the people around you. Take the principles and ideas shared in this work and apply them and I am sure wonderful things will happen. Finally, remember there is power in thoughts, as thoughts become words, words become actions, actions become habits, habits become a character, and character is transformed into your destiny. For that reason, be a guardian of your mind and heart.

"Carefully guard your thoughts because they are the source of true life." – Proverbs 4:23

Enjoy the ride!

Dr. Marcos A. Coronado Ortega
Vice Principal
Head of the Biomass and Bioenergy Laboratory
Autonomous University of Baja California

ACKNOWLEDGMENTS

"Thoughts are seeds for action." James Cheng

Why Reflection of Life is Essential? *was inspired by Brother James Cheng's statement* ***"Thoughts are seeds for action"*** *written in the Bible he left in my home.*

This statement has been etched on the tablet of my heart ever since.

The statement has become my credo of life, and it motivates me to put it into practice every time I come up with a new thought or an idea.

This practice ultimately led me to become a leading Singapore inventor with more than 25 filed patents, inventor of more than 500 products, one of Singapore's most inspiring entrepreneurs, author of books, and publisher of more than 140 scientific journals.

Through his ministry, he led many to Jesus as the first missionary from the Cheng clan.

The Lord has blessed him with success as a businessman, and he is a great witness for Jesus.

I would like to express my sincere gratitude to my beloved brother James Cheng for the statement he made. Once again, the statement above inspired this book.

My sincere thanks go out to you, bro.

Regards
Nelson Cheng

ABOUT THE AUTHOR

The author is the founder and chairman of the Magna Group, which encompasses Magna International, Magna Chemical Canada Inc, Magna Australia Pvt Ltd, and Lupromax International Pte Ltd. In addition, he is a senior honorary research fellow at the Autonomous University of Baja California.

One of the leading inventors in Singapore, he has filed more than twenty-five patents and more than fifteen trademarks both locally and internationally.

A total of more than 500 products have been invented by him including Heat-activated technology (HAT) lubricants, Vapor biocorrosion inhibitors (VBCI), Molecular Reaction Surface Technology (MRST), Colloidal Corrosion Inhibitors (CCI), Silver Nanoparticles Hospital Grade Disinfectants to combat hospital-acquired infections (HAIs) and more.

Over 230 of his inventions have received NATO Stock Numbers and have been marketed in more than 30 countries.

He has won numerous international awards for his packaging inventions, including the World Packaging Association's (WPA) President God Award, several World Packaging Excellence Awards, numerous Asia Packaging Federation (APF) Awards for packaging excellence, and many Singapore Star Awards for sustainable packaging.

Among his achievements is the Lupromax EA engine oil additive. This additive has been incorporated into the Indonesia World Record Museum after running cars and motorcycles without lubrication for 280 kilometers and 8 hours. Pioneer of the Legionella-X disinfectant, which kills 100% of the H5N1 Avian Flu Virus.

As an author and editor, he has authored four books: Vappro VBCI-The Solution to Corrosion Control, Legionella-X Disinfectants- Fighting Infectious Diseases, and Vappro VBCI Mothballing Reference Book, Turning Problems into Opportunities.

Having published 140 research papers and technical journals, in journals such as the National Association of Corrosion Engineers (NACE), International Journal of Emerging Technology and Advanced Engineering (IJETAE), International Journal of Current Trends in Engineering & Technology (IJCTET), Cambridge University Press, Academia.edu, ResearchGate, Intech Open, and co-authored books on anticorrosion and combating infectious diseases, as well as the mothballing of onshore and offshore equipment.

Among his many awards, he was the first Singaporean to win the 2020 World Packaging Star and the President Gold Award for Green and Sustainability Products.

Winner of the 2020 Asia Packaging and Singapore Star Packaging Awards for Green Packaging, 2015 Winner of the Asia Packaging Award, Top 10 Most Inspiring Entrepreneur 2015, Winner of the Global Star, Asia Star and Singapore Star Packaging Awards 2014, 2015, 2016, 2017, 2014, Top Entrepreneur Award-Singapore Small Medium Business Association, Asia Excellence Award 2014, and Top 20 Innovation Award 2013 from Small Medium Business Association.

Member of the National Association of Research Fellows (NARF) Australia, Society of Tribologists and Lubrication Engineers (STLE), American Chemical Society (ACS), World Corrosion Organization (WCO), and European Federation of Corrosion (EFC). Served on the committee of the Singapore Packaging Council.

"A man was born with the capability of creating and manifesting things not possible before he arrived." - Nelson Cheng

FEW WORDS FROM
THE AUTHOR

If I could give each of you a gift, it would be this book—*Reflection of Life.* More than thirty-five years of invaluable life experience are condensed in this book. We know that knowledge can be imparted, whereas experience needs to be acquired. However, a wise and receptive person can learn from the experience of others without going through the normal learning curve and avoid unnecessary pitfalls. *Reflection of Life* was written as a gift from me to those who are struggling in life because of a lack of self-reflection on life. Probably the only book that neatly summarises hundreds of key points, essential messages, with inspirational quotes and pictures.

Nelson Cheng

CONTENTS

1
C H A P T E R

Introduction to Reflection of Life

Have you ever wondered why many people suffer the same problems repeatedly?

This book aims to provoke readers to constantly reflect on their lives regularly to keep the same problems from recurring.

If our lives are plagued by the same problems more than once, it was only because we act without reflecting on their root causes, or we just reflect without taking any concrete action to resolve them.

Essentially, self-reflection is taking the time to think about, meditate on, evaluate, and give serious consideration to your behaviours, thoughts, attitudes, motivations, and desires. It entails the process of examining why the same problems are repeated.in itself. It involves your thoughts, emotions, and motivations and determining the why behind them.

By reflecting on your life on a personal level, you can analyse it from both a macro and micro perspective. The overall trajectory of your life can be evaluated at a macro level. If you have a clear understanding of where you are heading, you can adjust as necessary to ensure that you are satisfied with the direction.

A disciplined and intentional approach to self-reflection is required. Taking the time to think and ponder about your life requires you to pause from the chaos of your day-to-day existence, which is not easy for most people. However, it is an extremely valuable skill to acquire to eradicate same problems from reoccurring.

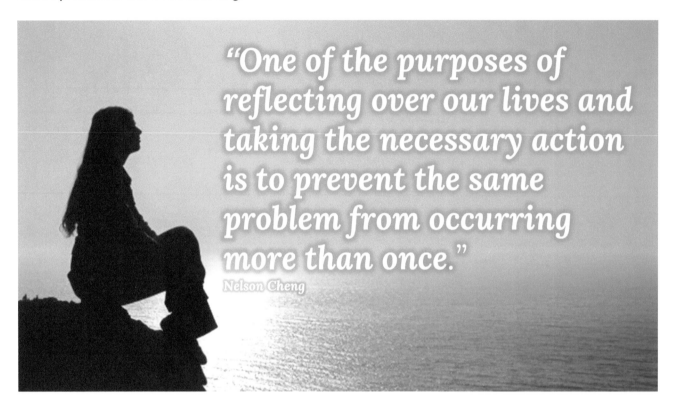

"One of the purposes of reflecting over our lives and taking the necessary action is to prevent the same problem from occurring more than once."
Nelson Cheng

In *Reflection of Life*, the author gathered more than three hundred inspirational quotes reflecting on his life journey as he considered how he overcame many difficulties with the help of God. He developed several inventions, industrial solutions, and innovations based on the principles he embraced.

The book can be read without reading from page to page; if you are interested in a particular chapter, just flip to it. For each section, there are real-life, proven inspirational quotes that will help you overcome obstacles in your way. Relevant pictures will be displayed alongside the inspirational quotes. As the old saying goes, 'A picture paints a thousand words' or 'A picture is worth a thousand words.

The book *Reflection of Life* contains a variety of sections that reflect individual needs depending on the phase of life the reader is in. Let's focus on the four distinct phases of life—namely, childhood, adolescence, adulthood, and senior years—for the sake of simplicity.

Childhood

We live in a constantly changing world. Throughout our society, every generation has faced different challenges as they grew up depending on the culture in which they were raised. Kids today face a set of challenges that are quite different from any other generation that has come before.

The primary cause of this is the increasing globalisation of our world. There has never been so much information and accessibility at our fingertips—a wonderful thing, but also a challenge that parents and their children must navigate with caution. The following are a few of the challenges kids face that adults never have to face:

Maintaining a routine

A typical school day is full of breaks, changes, and various types of learning. The school routine extends beyond its four walls. Kids must be awake by a certain time, fed, showered, and on the bus before school starts. The priority after school is homework and food. Schooling involves a lot of routines. Routines play an important role in the social development of a child. In a safe environment, they build skills, become comfortable around the world, and prepare for school challenges.

Cyberbullying

Cyberbullying is a very difficult thing to escape when the internet shapes a child's social and personal identity so strongly. To shut down the computer and ignore the bullying may seem like an easy solution, but it would be like telling the previous generation that because they were bullied, they should give up going to the park. Our kids meet online and on social media just like they did at parks or malls in previous generations.

There can be malicious acts committed online too. The online world can be dangerous because of the ability to say anything or to be anyone; it can be used to spread rumours and to say things that ordinarily wouldn't be said in public.

Cyberbullying is a serious issue that most schools and institutions deal with. Schools are one of the best ways to stop bullying along with many bullying and kids' helplines.

Adolescence

Teenagers have a hard time finding work, as they often look for casual jobs. If inappropriate content is posted on a social media account containing the teen's employer, or if the teen is dressed in a work uniform, it could bring the company into disrepute.

Adulthood

At this point in your life, you begin to accumulate responsibilities. It is the beginning of our need to make an impact on the world. Adulthood is a time of growth as families are formed and identities are formed through success at home and at work.

Adulthood may bring the following experiences:

- creating new desires and aspirations; the goal in the current stage of life is different from the goal of years past
- health changes
- increase in the size of the family
- greater awareness of spirituality
- distancing from society/reality, known as the midlife crisis

Senior years

We become aware of the last stage of our lives as we grow older. This can be a time when we slow down and reflect on what is important. Seniors must feel respected and valued.

The Maslow's hierarchy of needs

It doesn't matter where we are in our lives; these are the basic needs of every person. In every stage of a person's life, from infancy to death, various milestones should be celebrated. Enjoy that progression from one stage to the next as your needs and those around you change. You only get one shot at it.

The idea that human needs are arranged in order is widely held.

Physiological needs—among the most fundamental. All these things are necessary to sustain life, including air, water, food, shelter, and sleep. After a person's biological needs are met, they can move on to other needs.

Safety needs—keeping yourself safe from the elements by observing the laws that govern your community.

Need of belonging/love—a sense of belonging is created by intimacy and friendship. Need for intimacy and need for friendship are two forms of belonging.

Esteem needs—earning success, independence, and self-respect. Having confidence in one's ability, independence, and self-respect are all characteristics of self-esteem.

Self-actualisation—achieving self-actualisation entails trying to understand your place in the world more and realise your own entail; seeking personal growth and developing a greater understanding of your place in the world.

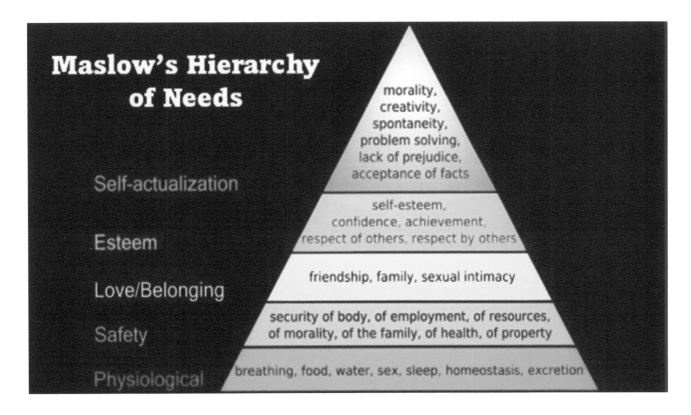

The only way for us to understand what stage of life we are in is to reflect on our lives regularly. By doing so, we will avoid the pitfalls of life without needing to encounter the normal process of learning and will thus be able to cope with them more effectively.

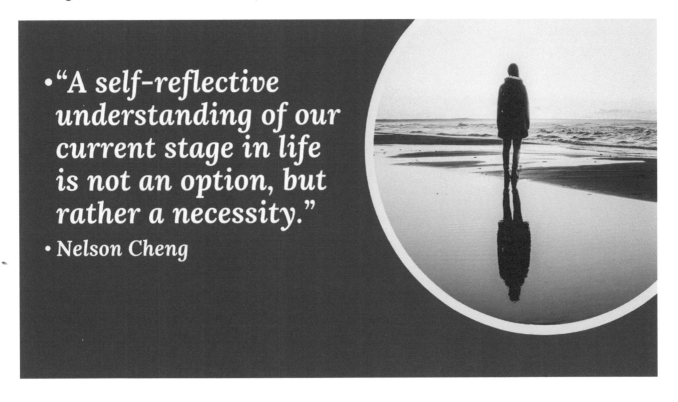

The ability to learn from mistakes and successes comes from self-awareness. Growing comes from self-awareness.
—Nelson Cheng

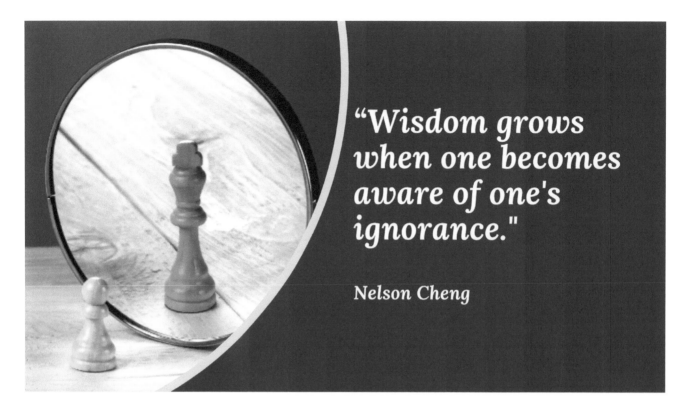

"Wisdom grows when one becomes aware of one's ignorance."

Nelson Cheng

"Self-Reflection helps in eliminating one's ignorance."

"Having a self-reflective mindset helps in removing ignorance."

"Being humble is being aware of who you are."

Nelson Cheng

2
CHAPTER
The Importance of Self-Reflection

The unexamined life is not worth living.
—Socrates

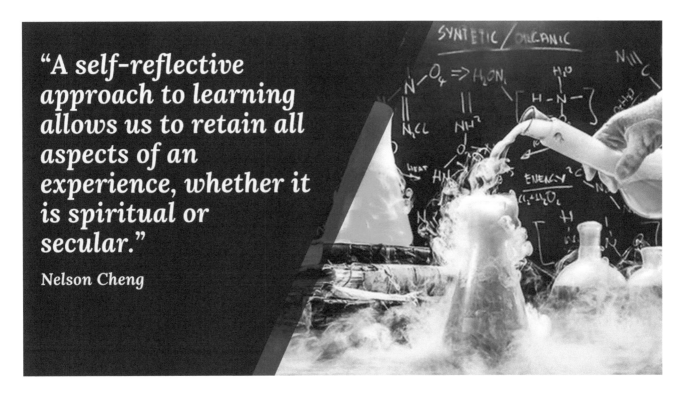

"A self-reflective approach to learning allows us to retain all aspects of an experience, whether it is spiritual or secular."

Nelson Cheng

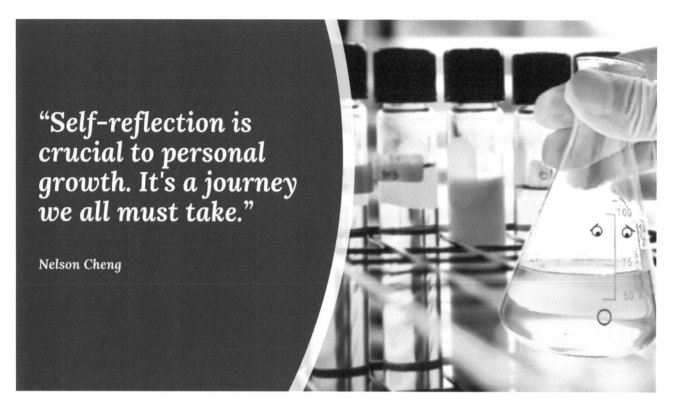

> "Self-reflection is crucial to personal growth. It's a journey we all must take."
>
> *Nelson Cheng*

"*If you do not take time to reflect on yourself, you will not grow* "

What is self-reflection?

In a nutshell, self-reflection is taking the time to examine, think about, evaluate, and give serious consideration to your behaviours, thoughts, attitudes, motivations, and desires. A process of in-depth analysis of your thoughts, emotions, and motivations to figure out the why behind them.

From both a macro and a micro perspective, it provides an in-depth analysis of your life. It is possible to evaluate the overall trajectory of your life at a macro level. This way, you can see where you are heading, determine whether you are happy with the direction, and make necessary adjustments.

The importance of self-reflection

The Importance of Self-reflection

"In the absence of self-reflection, we simply go from one thing to another, as if nothing has changed."
Nelson Cheng

The most effective reflection involves the conscious consideration and analysis of beliefs and actions for learning. During reflection, the brain has an opportunity to pause amidst the chaos, untangle and sort through observations and experiences, consider multiple possible interpretations, and create meaning. In this way, meaning is transformed into learning, which can then inform future actions and mindsets.

In the absence of self-reflection, we simply go from one thing to another, as if nothing has changed. We do not pause for thought to try to understand and determine what is working and what isn't. When we don't determine what needs to be done, we get stuck.

A lack of reflection could lead us to stay in a job we don't like or to stay in a relationship that isn't working out well.

When we fail to reflect, we just keep running, trying to keep up with things even when things aren't going well. This sometimes feels like floating along without any direction. Even if the results were not what we expected, we kept doing the same things.

How self-reflection can benefit you

While taking time to reflect is challenging, it can be very rewarding. We often find it difficult to take the time to step back and consider what truly matters. Nevertheless, there are numerous wonderful benefits of self-reflection, and we should all make time for it.

Self-reflection allows us to express the emotions and feelings that we have about our past successes or failures so that we can learn from them as we continue to move forward to the new tomorrow.

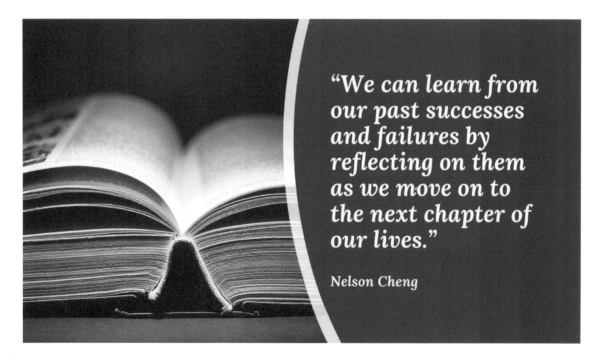

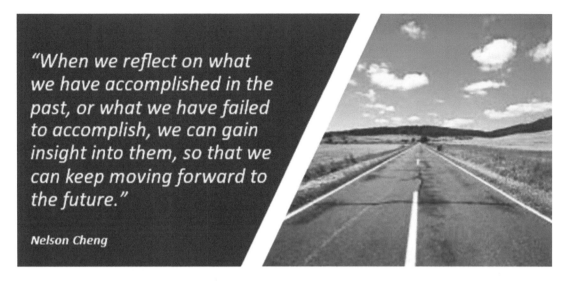

"When we reflect on what we have accomplished in the past, or what we have failed to accomplish, we can gain insight into them, so that we can keep moving forward to the future."

Nelson Cheng

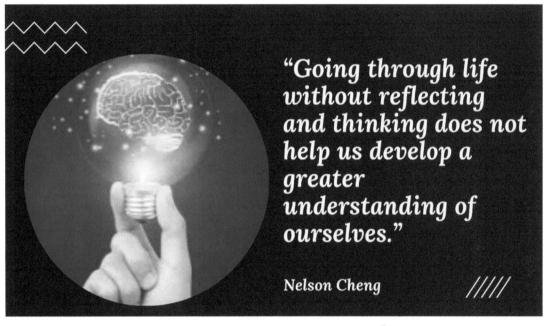

"Going through life without reflecting and thinking does not help us develop a greater understanding of ourselves."

Nelson Cheng

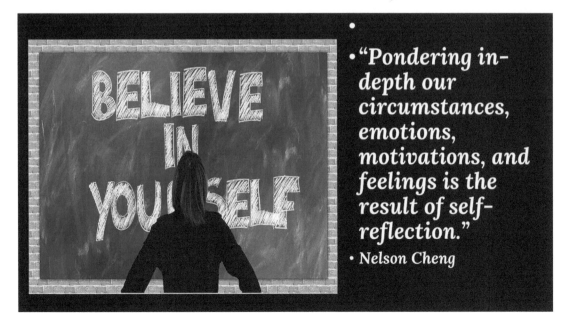

• "Pondering in-depth our circumstances, emotions, motivations, and feelings is the result of self-reflection."
• Nelson Cheng

It allows one to gain a new perspective.

New Perspective

It allows one to gain a new perspective.

You can lose sight of what matters most when emotions cloud your judgement. You may perceive certain things as bigger and worse than they are.

Through self-reflection, you can gain perspective on the issues that matter and the ones you can ignore. Self-reflection provides insight into events and the meaning surrounding them.

It improves your response efficiency.

Generally, we just react to whatever situation arises. The result is that we can say or do things we regret later. We don't give our words and actions the attention they deserve when we're reacting.

When we reflect, we can consider the consequences of our words and actions. It also enables you to consider how to act in each situation in the most effective, most helpful manner.

It facilitates the process of learning and understanding.

We don't develop a deeper understanding of our lives when we go through life without reflecting and thinking, never pausing to consider what valuable lessons we might learn; we just move from one thing to another.

Reflecting on our experiences, on the other hand, allows us to reflect on and evaluate them. The act of contemplation encourages us to ponder our circumstances, emotions, motivations, and feelings in depth. Through contemplation, we can lead a more holistic, integrated, and fulfilling life.

It provides a process for self-assessment.

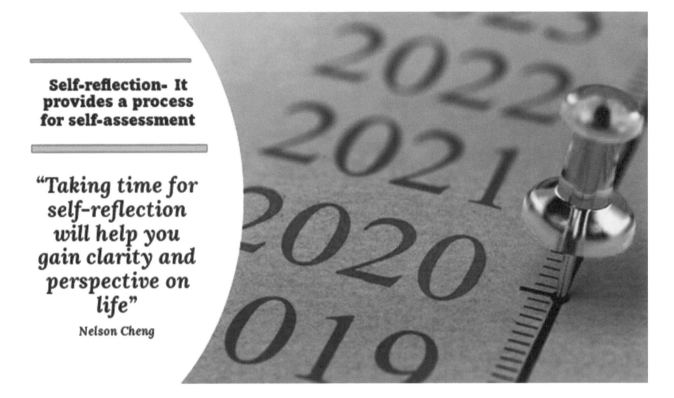

Self-reflection- It provides a process for self-assessment

"Taking time for self-reflection will help you gain clarity and perspective on life"

Nelson Cheng

So how exactly do you reflect on yourself?

This self-reflection exercise can be carried out using a journal. Take your time answering these questions by writing them out. Take your time. Think about it. Consider what matters most to you.

Taking time for self-reflection will help you gain clarity and perspective on life.

In what way can you most effectively reflect on your life?

Start by deciding the time you will look back on. Would you rather reflect on the last week? a month ago? the year before? the last five years?

Taking stock of what happened is a good place to start. You will find this step easier if you already keep a journal, as well as a good reminder of why you should do so.

Examine your planner, journal, and photos and mark out the highs and lows.

Recalling low points can be difficult, but it is also an excellent way to gain clarity and grow.

Consider whether each low point was within your control.

If yes, think about what you could do differently next time.

If not, consider your options for finding peace with it.

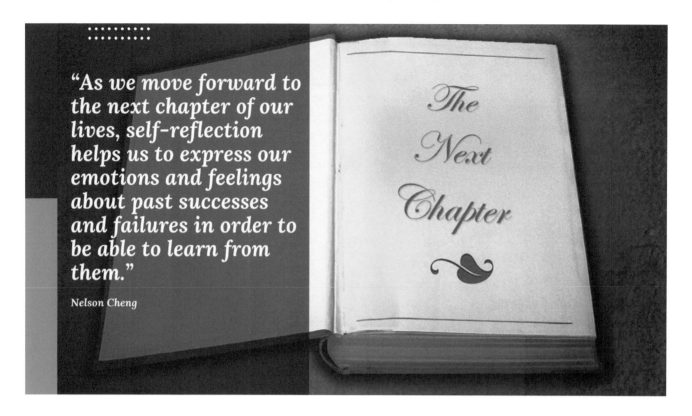

"As we move forward to the next chapter of our lives, self-reflection helps us to express our emotions and feelings about past successes and failures in order to be able to learn from them."

Nelson Cheng

Self-reflection encompasses our total being

Self-reflection Encompasses Our Total Being

"A man can only be whole when his mind, body, and soul is in harmony." -Nelson Cheng

Wholeness can only be achieved if the mind, body, and soul work together. – Nelson Cheng

A thorough self-reflection is beneficial to the mind, body, and soul. When you have conducted a thorough self-reflection, your mind feels clearer and more engaged, and you are intellectually challenged as you move forward into the next phase of your life.

When you have resolved all the unsettled matters through self-reflection, you will find your body feeling healthy, nourished, and strong.

When you are at peace, your soul can act in harmony with the world around you.

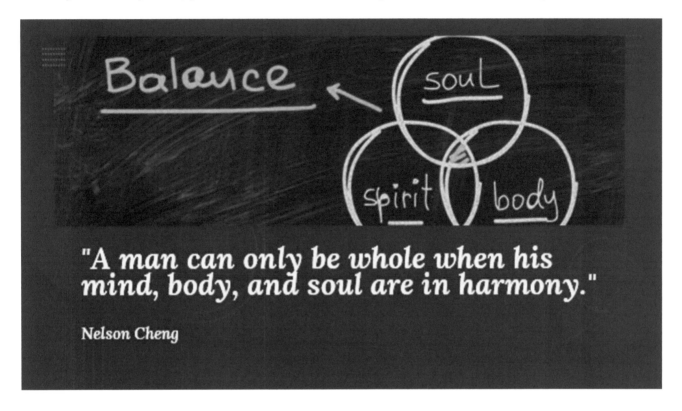

Wholeness can only be achieved if the mind, body, and soul work together.

Why do people fail to reflect on themselves?

Self-reflection is not common because people have numerous reasons not to do so. These are three common excuses for reluctance to reflect on oneself:

Having problems with the process

The process of reflection requires a lot of things that one doesn't like to do. It requires setting aside time from our daily routine and discipline. Most people often find it difficult to slow down, accept uncertainty and curiosity, make accommodations for messiness and inefficiency, and take personal responsibility as part of the reflection process. Though the process can help uncover valuable insights and even lead to breakthroughs, it can also create uncomfortable emotions, vulnerabilities, defensiveness, and irritation.

A failure to see a positive return on investment (ROI)

In early careers, many are taught to invest where they can achieve a positive ROI—results that show how the contribution of time, talent, or money paid off. Reflection sometimes doesn't have an immediate return on investment—especially when compared with other uses of a leader's time.

Don't like the results

In taking the time to reflect, an individual can see both one's strengths and shortcomings. Some individuals may dismiss their strengths, while others may dislike their shortcomings. Some people get so defensive that they fail to learn anything, and so the results are not beneficial.

How to begin self-reflection?

Make a choice that matches your preferences for reflection. For many, writing in a journal is the best method to reflect. Alternatively, you could talk with a colleague if that sounds better. You can choose whatever approach you want if it's reflective and not just a conversation about the latest sporting event or a complaint about a colleague. Whether alone or with a partner, you can write, talk, or think as you sit, walk, bike, or stand.

Time slot. Most leaders plan their days based on their schedules. Plan your time to reflect and be committed to keeping it. If you find yourself avoiding or skipping it, reflect on that!

Make small steps. Start with ten minutes of reflection if an hour seems too much. Researchers Teresa Amabile and her colleagues found that progress on daily tasks drove positive emotions and motivation at work. Encourage yourself to make progress, no matter how small.

Don't hesitate. Review your questions again. Sit calmly. Reflect. Consider multiple perspectives. Take the opposite approach to what you initially believed. Organise your thoughts. The key is to think and examine your thoughts, not to like or agree with them all.

Get help if you need it. Reflection is difficult for most leaders because of a lack of desire, time, experience, or skills. You may want to consider working with a colleague, therapist, or coach to assist you in making the time, listening carefully, reflecting, and holding yourself accountable.

Reflection is challenging; it has a significant impact.

Follow effective action with quiet reflection. From the quiet
reflection will come even more effective action.
—Peter Drucker

3
CHAPTER

Reflection on the Purpose of Leadership

An important purpose of leadership is to make a positive contribution to improving society or humanity.
—Nelson Cheng

Leadership is nothing if we do not contribute to the betterment of humanity or society at large. If leaders are not making a positive impact on their societies, then what is the point of having the smartest or most educated leader?

What does a leader mean in basic terms?

A leader is someone who directs or controls the activities of a group.

A leader is someone who commands or leads a group, an organisation, or a country.

Leaders are defined differently over time. According to the dictionary, a leader is someone who directs or controls the activities of a group.

What does it take to be a true leader?

What is a true leader?

"A true leader inspires others and leads with confidence and integrity, creating a positive team dynamic that produces results."

Nelson Cheng

Leaders are individuals who take the initiative to accomplish things within their groups or organisations. Oftentimes, they are the first to take things on and complete projects. To achieve their vision of success, good leaders often see how it will look in the future and then decide how to organise themselves and others to achieve it. While doing so, they inspire others and lead with confidence and integrity, creating a positive team dynamic that produces results.

What are the traits of a quasi-leader?

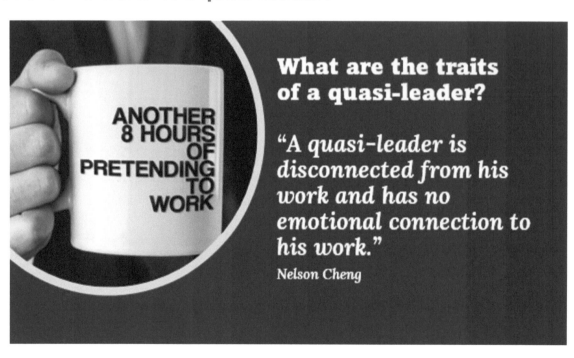

What are the traits of a quasi-leader?

"A quasi-leader is disconnected from his work and has no emotional connection to his work."

Nelson Cheng

ANOTHER 8 HOURS OF PRETENDING TO WORK

The reason for being a leader in any organisation has nothing to do with our egos or our legacy; it is about serving the people who are under us and improving their lives.
—Nelson Cheng

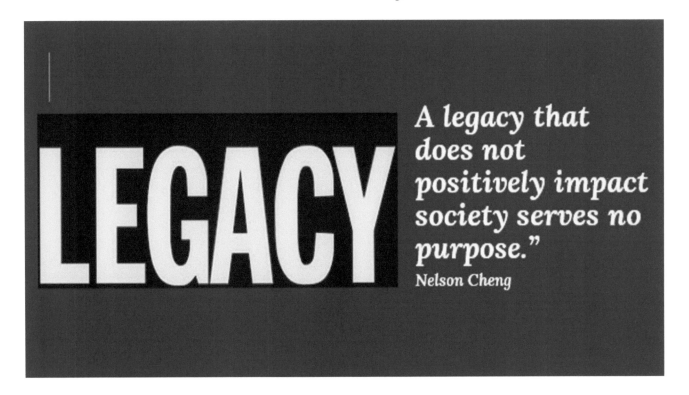

On the last days of my life, before I expire on earth, I will ask myself this question: What have I done for humanity?
—Nelson Cheng

On the last days of my life, before I expire on earth, I will ask myself these questions what have I done for humanity?

"What have done with the talents God has blessed me with?"

"How many people have I positively impacted?"

"Will God make this statement "Well done my good and faithful servant —?

Nelson Cheng

4
CHAPTER

Reflection on Life's Adversity and Resiliency

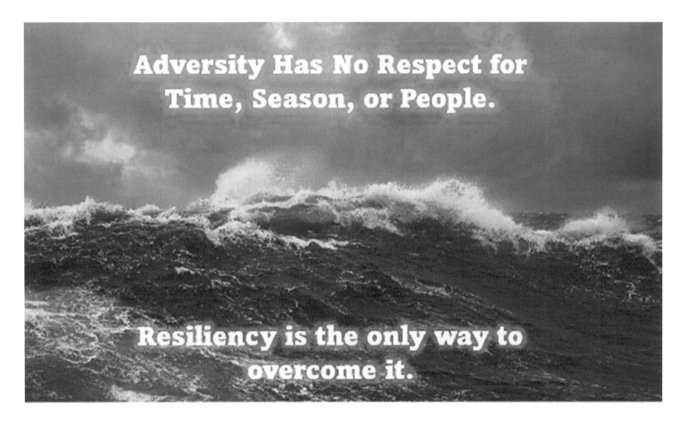

Adversity of life

Adversity has no respect for time, season, or people.
Resiliency is the only way to overcome it.
—Nelson Cheng

Adversity is a part of life for everyone, just at varying degrees and in different forms. The difficulties or misfortunes you face can be turned into positive opportunities if you take appropriate steps. The ability to be dedicated and motivated and to believe in oneself is crucial to improving one's life circumstances despite adversity.

There are many different types of adversities one can encounter throughout their life, and facing adversity can either make or break a person. Others may turn to drugs or alcohol to relieve the psychological burden of their hardships, or it may lead them to improve their life by finding ways to overcome their challenges.

Some of life's adversities include the following:

Physical adversity

A physical disability is one form of physical adversity. An athlete may suffer a career-ending injury that drastically alters their life trajectory, leading to physical adversity. Furthermore, those suffering from blindness, deafness, obesity, or chronic pain may have to struggle to lead a normal life because of the difficulties brought up by those ailments.

Mental adversity

An individual may be limited by a mental disorder or mental illness. When coping with mental adversity, seeking help from a physician, a psychologist, or a psychiatrist can make a lot of difference in one's life. A person seeks treatment to maintain their health and lead a normal life. Resilient people seek treatment more often than those who deny it.

Financial adversity

Among the many adversities facing our society and the rest of the world, financial adversity may be the most apparent. The inability to afford necessities makes it difficult to lead a happy life and can cause jealousy and anger.

Social adversity

Human interaction is crucial to our existence. If a person lacks social skills, he or she may have difficulty finding work, making friends, or maintaining a family unit. Improving these skills can be extremely beneficial.

Inspirational quote for overcoming adversity

Reflection of Life offers readers quotes based on the author's own life experiences and adversities. Reading this book can also increase your confidence, which helps you succeed in the future. Additionally, you will learn skills and strategies to help you overcome adversity when it strikes.

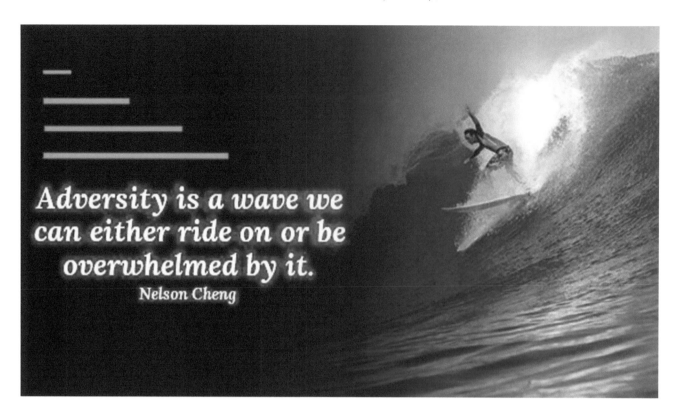

Adversity is a wave we can either ride on or be overwhelmed by it.
Nelson Cheng

To overcome adversity, you need to determine the cause and start working on solutions. Worrying about it will not make you any better; instead, it will make you less creative and affect your emotions. To surf on the crest of the wave of adversity requires seeking the direction and wisdom from God and then applying it.

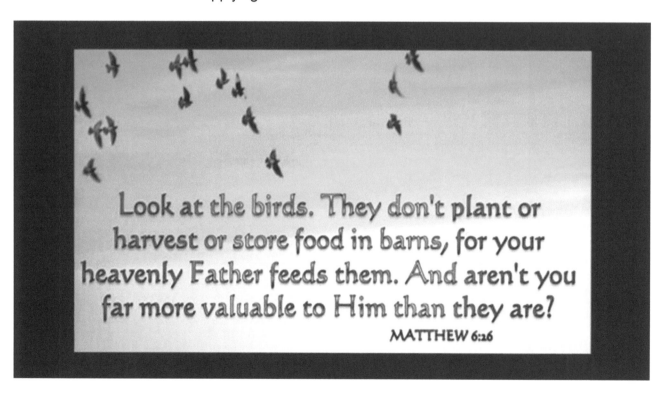

Look at the birds. They don't plant or harvest or store food in barns, for your heavenly Father feeds them. And aren't you far more valuable to Him than they are?
MATTHEW 6:26

And who of you by being worried can add a single hour to his life?
—Matthew 6:25

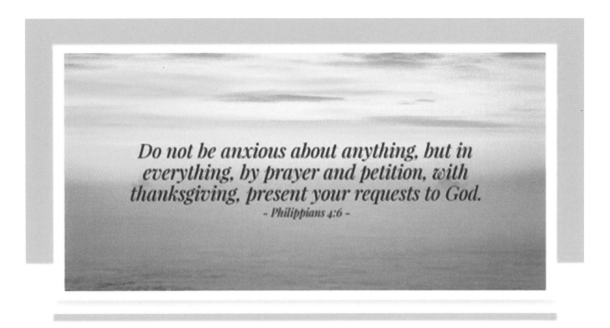

Do not be anxious about anything, but in everything, by prayer and petition, with thanksgiving, present your requests to God.
- Philippians 4:6 -

Don't worry about anything but present your requests to God in every situation by prayer and petition.

The importance of being an optimist when facing adversity in life

Adversities occur to everyone at some point, and one can be either the cause or the solution. When facing adversity, it is of paramount importance to find the best available possible solution to solve it based on your existing resources.

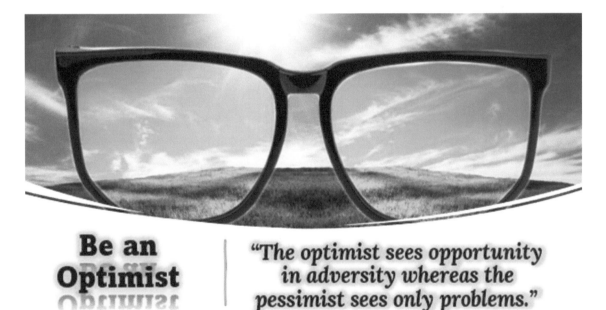

Be an Optimist | *"The optimist sees opportunity in adversity whereas the pessimist sees only problems."*

The optimist sees opportunity in adversity, whereas the pessimist sees only problems.
—Nelson Cheng

There are two sides to every coin, and life is all about perspective when facing adversity. If you put on the glasses of an optimist, you will see the green pasture; and if you wear the glasses of a pessimist, you will see only dried grass.

How to overcome adversity

"Preparedness is the key to overcoming adversity."
Nelson Cheng

Those who are prepared for an impending superstorm are likely to survive it.

The same is true for adversity. During an early January 2020 trip to Austria, when I heard about Covid-19 from a distributor in China, I notified my procurement department of the need to beef up raw materials and packaging materials to produce disinfectants.

Therefore, when Covid-19 arrived on the shores of Singapore, Magna was probably one of the companies that could produce more than three hundred thousand litres of disinfectant, while our competitors struggled to buy raw materials and packaging materials to produce disinfectant.

Health-care providers, governments, and the public eagerly sought out disinfectants and facial masks. Their prices skyrocketed. We even airfreighted our many pallets of disinfectants to many overseas distributors.

We had one of our best years because of well preparedness for Covid-19 in 2020, while many SMEs were winding up their businesses because of a lack of preparation for said adversity.

Preparing for STORM SEASON

"Those who expect the unexpected will be better prepared than those who do not expect it at all."

Nelson Cheng

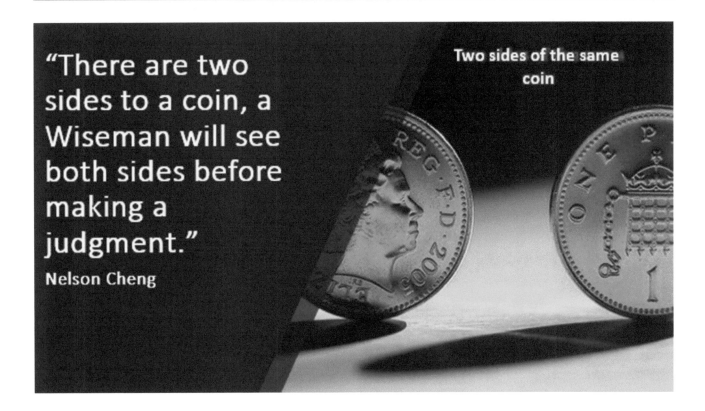

"There are two sides to a coin, a Wiseman will see both sides before making a judgment."

Nelson Cheng

Two sides of the same coin

Expect the unexpected

"To overcome adversity one must learn to expect the worse and meanwhile hope for the best."
–Nelson Cheng

Resiliency

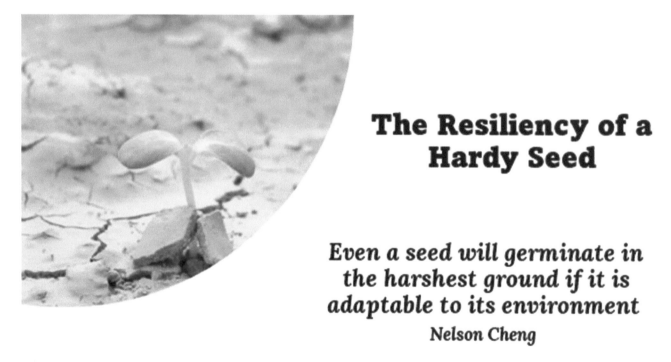

The Resiliency of a Hardy Seed

Even a seed will germinate in the harshest ground if it is adaptable to its environment
Nelson Cheng

Resiliency is simply being able to cope with adversity or adjust to change without much difficulty. Rather than being determined by a man's size or masculinity, resilience is determined by his mental strength. When confronted with adversity, a person's mental strength will determine whether he succeeds in overcoming it.

Resiliency

"Resiliency is not based on the size or the masculinity of the man but rather on the strength of his mind."

Nelson Cheng

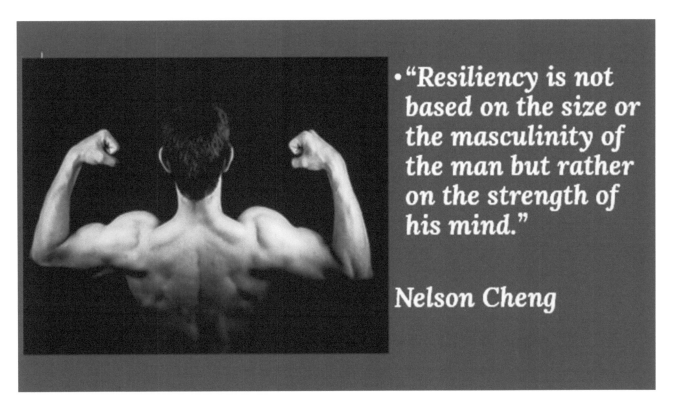

"Resiliency is not based on the size or the masculinity of the man but rather on the strength of his mind."

Nelson Cheng

The strength of his mental faculty determines whether a man will be able to overcome the adversity he is facing, not his size or his masculinity.
— Nelson Cheng

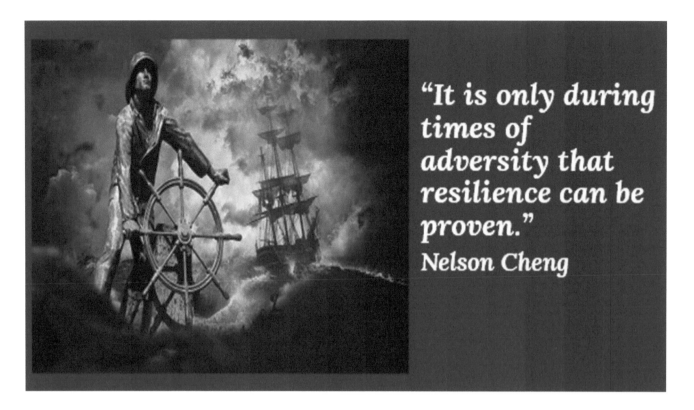

People become more resilient through adversity. Just like exercise is good for the body, adversity is good for the mind. Adversity is the platform on which resilience is built.

The fact that adversity strengthens resilience cannot be denied. Only when one has developed this paradigm will one be able to overcome adversity. A person's level of resilience correlates to the extent of adversity they face. Adversity will reveal a man's courage and resiliency.

Adversity in experiencing a broken relationship

Adversity on Relationship

"One cannot soar if he or she carries the baggage of hurts."

- Nelson Cheng

Life isn't always rosy from the perspective of family, friends, or colleagues; sometimes the relationship can turn sour. If there are any misunderstandings, do your best to resolve them; but sometimes the other party may not want to resolve them, so you must move on without your emotions being affected.

• "To soar in life, one has to check in his or her baggage of hurts into God's Cargo Compartments.

Nelson Cheng

5
CHAPTER

Reflection on Making a Difference with One's Life

Definition of making a difference

To make a difference is simply to do something that matters, which can help people or make the world a better place. Most people are unaware that they can each make a difference. This chapter intends to encourage and empower anyone to make a positive change in the world.

Anyone with a sound mind can contribute to their fellow man positively. One small act of kindness can make a huge difference in someone's life. When a drop of water is dropped, a ripple effect is created.

The ripple effects

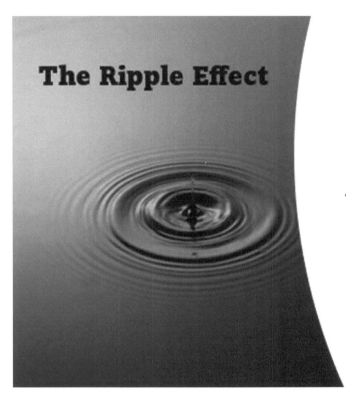

One Can a Difference

"Number one is a powerful number that should not be underestimated or trivialized. It is the beginning number of a billion." – Nelson Cheng

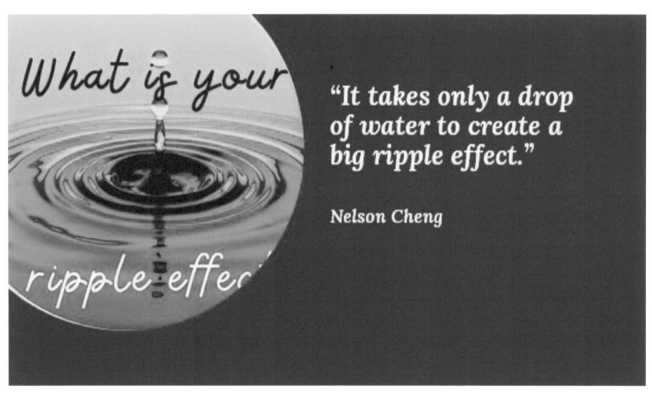

"It takes only a drop of water to create a big ripple effect."

Nelson Cheng

The secret to owning your big ripple effect is to keep doing anything that has a positive impact on one's life.
—Nelson Cheng

One can make a difference

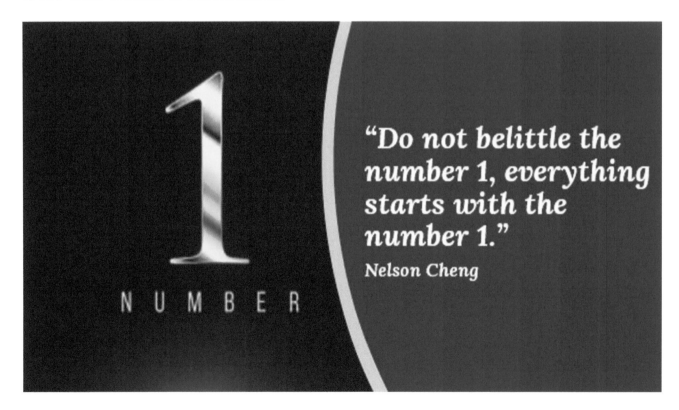

Never undervalue or trivialise the number one. It is the beginning of everything.
—Nelson Cheng

Number one is a powerful number that should not be underestimated or trivialised.
It is the beginning number of a billion.
—Nelson Cheng

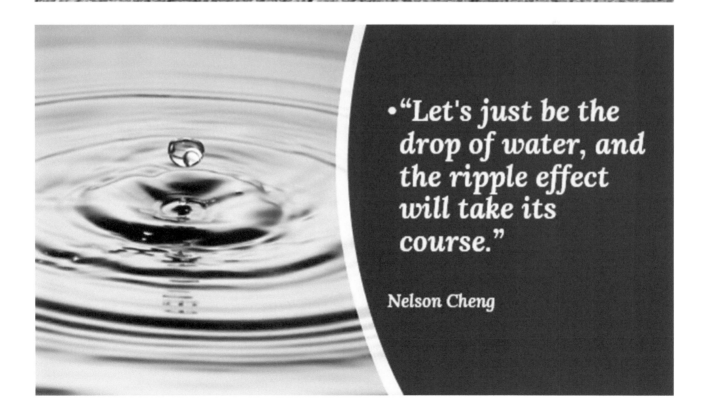

"Just Like Each Grain of Sand Contributes to Making of a Beach, Each Individual Can Make A Difference in a Society." –Nelson Cheng

It is every grain of sand that makes up the beach

•"Let's just be the drop of water, and the ripple effect will take its course."

Nelson Cheng

"One can make a difference, just keep doing what God has placed in your heart, it's a matter of time others will follow."

Nelson Cheng

By building the bridge, it makes a great difference in crossing the rapids

A person who makes a difference makes a situation better by doing the right thing.
—Nelson Cheng

Making a difference will result in a significant change of the situation and positively alter its circumstances.
—Nelson Cheng

"It only takes a spark to start the fire glowing"

Factors of
99 and 100

• "The difference between 99 and 100 is unit 1. It is unit 1 that separates 99 from 100."

• Nelson Cheng

Hence, each one of us can make a difference by doing something good for our society, country, and humanity.

Making a difference through leading

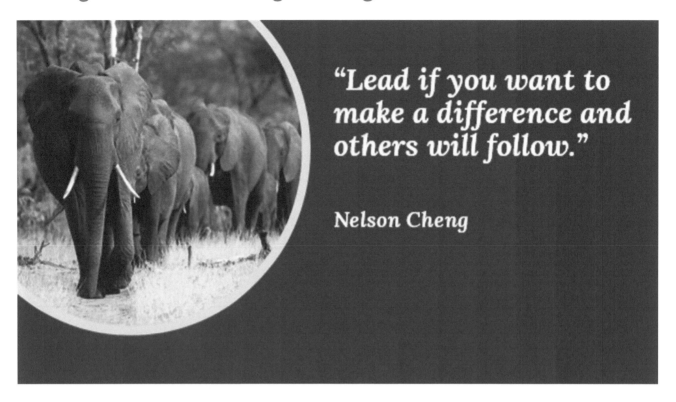

Leading by example can make a great difference for anyone in a leadership role, no matter what they are. Leading from the front can make a great difference when we have a leadership role in any capacity

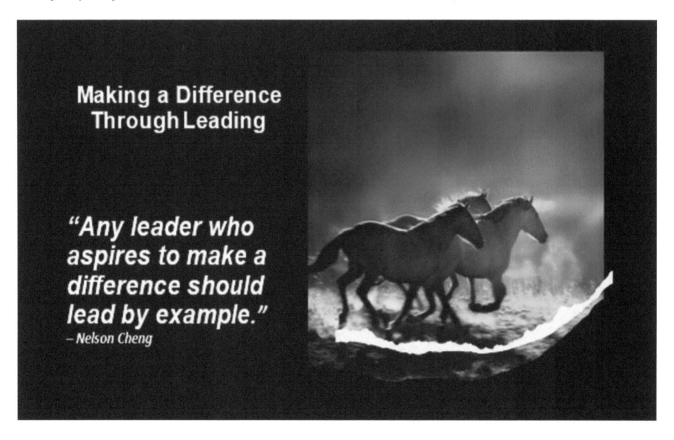

Anytime we lead by example, we make a big difference in our leadership position.
—Nelson Cheng

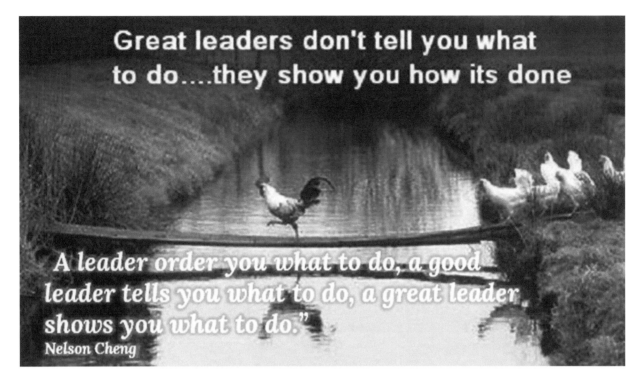

Any leader who aspires to make a difference should lead by example.
—Nelson Cheng

The true leader leads by example; the pseudo one tells you to do it.
—Nelson Cheng

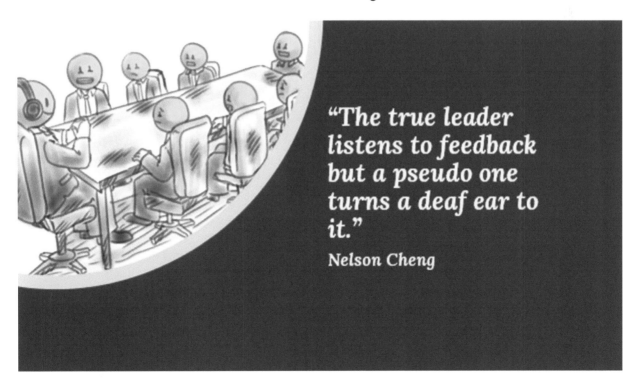

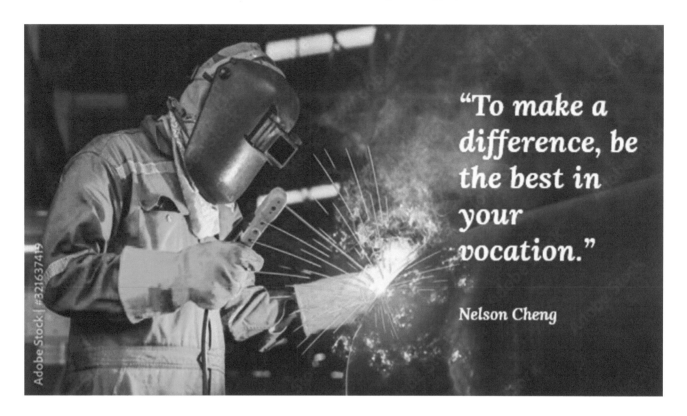

"To make a difference, be the best in your vocation."

Nelson Cheng

6
CHAPTER

Reflection on Little Details of Life

Life is full of details that we often neglect. In our busy lives, we often ignore seemingly insignificant details that seem inconsequential in contrast to the major concerns of life. We must focus on the little details to stand out from the crowd and distinguish ourselves from the masses.

Hence, our ability to differentiate ourselves from the masses and stand out from the crowds depends on paying attention to little details that others usually overlook.

If you want to engage the reader's senses and bring mental and emotional pleasure while reviewing a business proposal, a product presentation, or writing an article, you must include sensory details as well as seeing, feeling, hearing, and so on.

"Masses of people focus on the major details, while few pay attention to the little details."

Nelson Cheng

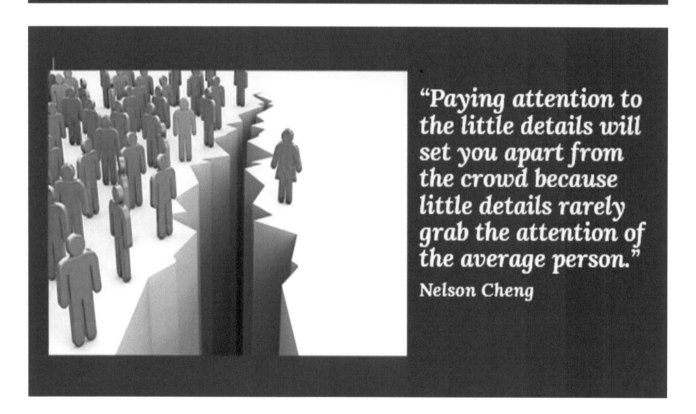

"Paying attention to the little details will set you apart from the crowd because little details rarely grab the attention of the average person."

Nelson Cheng

A great leader has an eye for both the mega picture without losing sight of the little details.
—Nelson Cheng

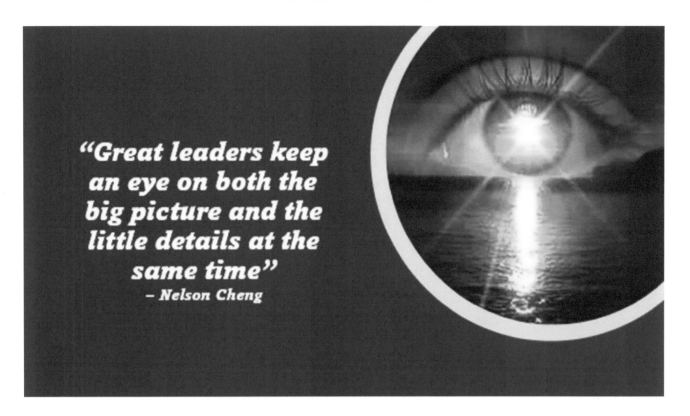

"Great leaders keep an eye on both the big picture and the little details at the same time"
– Nelson Cheng

"The little details rarely capture the attention of the average person, so if you take the time to pay attention to them, you will stand out from the crowd."

Nelson Cheng

The difference between a me-too product and a product of exception is the little details.
—Nelson Cheng

Most people focus on major details, whereas few care about minor details.
—Nelson Cheng

A great thing is when the little details are added to a good thing.
—Nelson Cheng

"A good photo produces a clear picture, whereas a great photo produces a clear picture and all its little details." -Nelson Cheng

Reflection on Little Details of Life

"The difference between good photography and great photography are in the little details" -Nelson Cheng

What separates great from the good is the extra little details.
—Nelson Cheng

The little details are what make the difference between good and great.
—Nelson Cheng

"Almost no one is concerned with the little details, hence, if you pay attention to the little details, you distance yourself from the masses."
Nelson Cheng

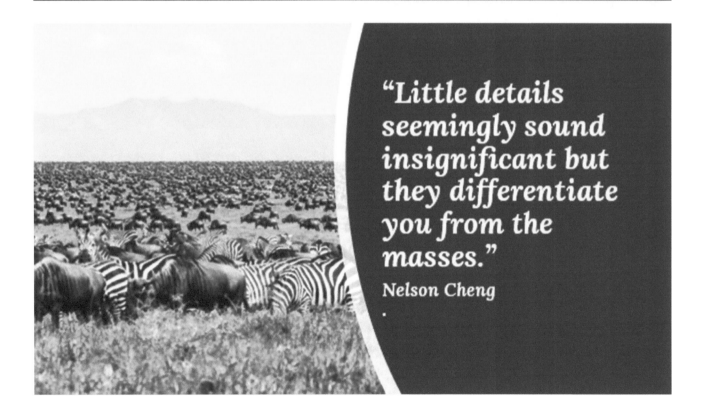

"Little details seemingly sound insignificant but they differentiate you from the masses."
Nelson Cheng

7

CHAPTER

Reflection on Ideas and Seeds

Definition of an idea and seed

Ideas are thoughts, plans, or suggestions about what to do.

Rather than holding on to ideas, we should pursue them.
—Nelson Cheng

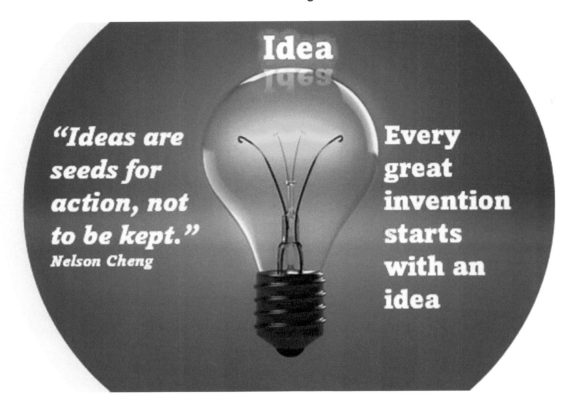

Seeds are the fertilised, ripened ovules of flowering plants that contain an embryo and are capable of germination to produce a new plant.

"Seeds of action, not ideas, are the seeds of innovation."

Nelson Cheng

"Unless seeds are sown, they will remain like seeds."

Nelson Cheng

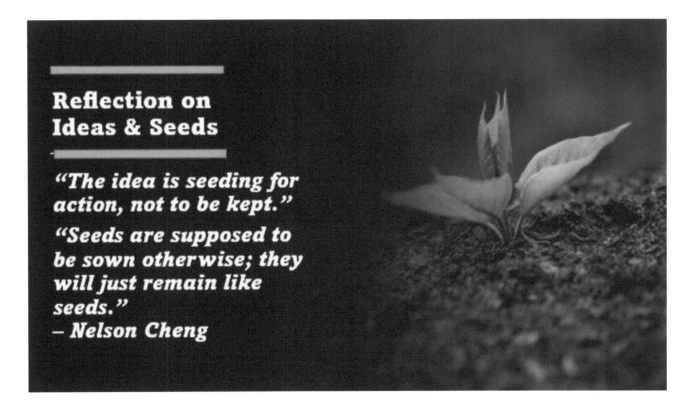

Reflection on Ideas & Seeds

"The idea is seeding for action, not to be kept."

"Seeds are supposed to be sown otherwise; they will just remain like seeds."
— Nelson Cheng

"The world will be a better place to live with more people talking about ideas instead of talking about people."
Nelson Cheng

Every great invention starts with an idea. Let's spend more time talking about it.
—Nelson Cheng

Reflection on Ideas and Seeds

"If the invention is for the betterment of humanity, no matter how big or small it is, it is a great invention." – Nelson Cheng

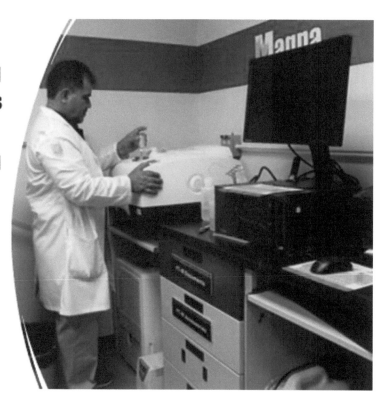

8

CHAPTER

Reflection on Time

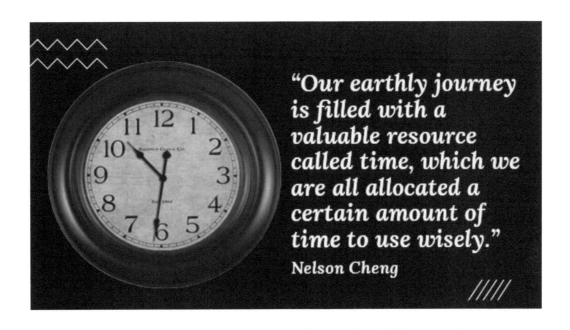

"Our earthly journey is filled with a valuable resource called time, which we are all allocated a certain amount of time to use wisely."

Nelson Cheng

Psalm 90:12, 14

So teach us to number our days, that we may gain a heart of wisdom. Satisfy us in the morning with your loving kindness, that we may rejoice and be glad all our days.

The Reflection on Time

The value of time cannot be measured in money. Time is irreplaceable; it cannot be bought with money. Time is an invaluable resource. As we journey through this world, we are all allotted a certain amount of time, which we should use wisely.

We must make the most of the limited amount of time we have here on earth by making our lives count.

Reflection on Time

"Time is precious do not squander it away."
Nelson Cheng

"The greatest spendthrifts on earth are those who squandered their precious time away."
Nelson Cheng

The most wasteful people on earth waste their precious time.
—Nelson Cheng

Reflection on Time

"Do what you have to do today, as tomorrow may never come."
Nelson Cheng

The thief of opportunity is procrastination.
—Nelson Cheng

We should do what needs to be done today, as tomorrow may never come.

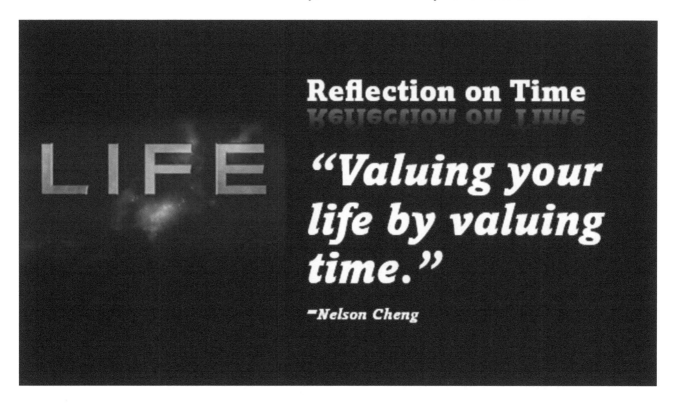

LIFE

Reflection on Time

"Valuing your life by valuing time."

—Nelson Cheng

Your life will become more valuable when you value your precious time.

The key to valuing your life is valuing time.

Reflection on time based on Ecclesiastes 3:1–8

Understand the seasons of life by understanding God's sovereignty.

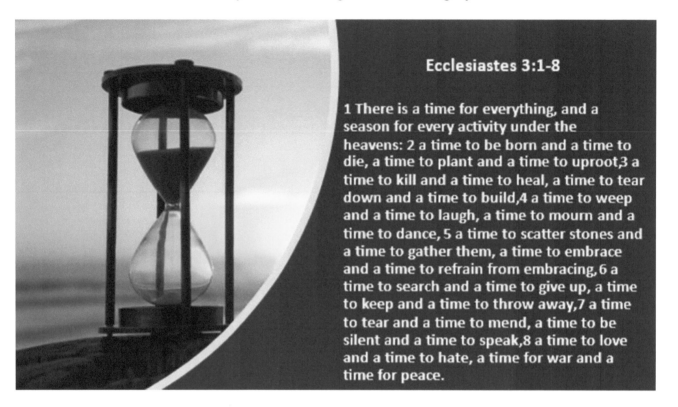

Ecclesiastes 3:1-8

1 There is a time for everything, and a season for every activity under the heavens: 2 a time to be born and a time to die, a time to plant and a time to uproot,3 a time to kill and a time to heal, a time to tear down and a time to build,4 a time to weep and a time to laugh, a time to mourn and a time to dance, 5 a time to scatter stones and a time to gather them, a time to embrace and a time to refrain from embracing,6 a time to search and a time to give up, a time to keep and a time to throw away,7 a time to tear and a time to mend, a time to be silent and a time to speak,8 a time to love and a time to hate, a time for war and a time for peace.

A **t**ime for **e**verything

The seasons of spring, summer, autumn, and winter metaphorically reflect our lives because each season has its beauty and challenges that impact our stance and perspective. We can indicate their advantages and disadvantages easily, but what matters most is what focus the beholder places on them at the appropriate time.

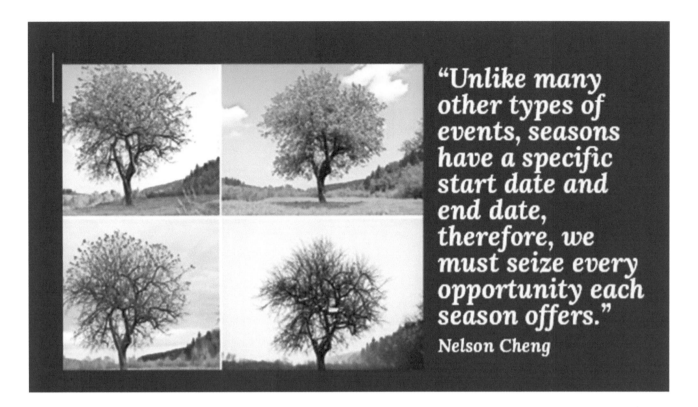

"Unlike many other types of events, seasons have a specific start date and end date, therefore, we must seize every opportunity each season offers."

Nelson Cheng

Likewise, we should also take advantage of seasons of blessing and harvest when the Lord provides. There is nothing wrong with celebrating a financial windfall, a child's birth, a decision of salvation, continued good health, conquests, accomplishments and graduations, time with those we love, etc.

9
CHAPTER

Reflection on Family–
Its Importance

The Importance of Family Unit

In this chapter on *Reflection of Life*, the importance of the family unit is particularly stressed. Families are the foundation of a healthy society.

The family is the fundamental social unit of all human societies, and healthy individuals within healthy families are the basis of a healthy society. Creating a positive environment for all families is in everyone's best interest.

A sad sight is seeing someone disown their parents, children, or siblings because of misunderstandings or unresolved conflicts.

Family and kinship have been well taught by my parents to me and my siblings. As the saying goes, 'Blood is thicker than water.' When used as a metaphor, a person's family takes precedence over anyone else's relationships, needs, or matters. Family is regarded as more valuable than anything. We are therefore more likely to overlook an offence among our family members if we truly comprehend the wisdom of the saying.

"We all need a family, a clan, a tribe, whatever you call it. Regardless of whose clan you belong to, you must have one because no man is an island."

Nelson Cheng

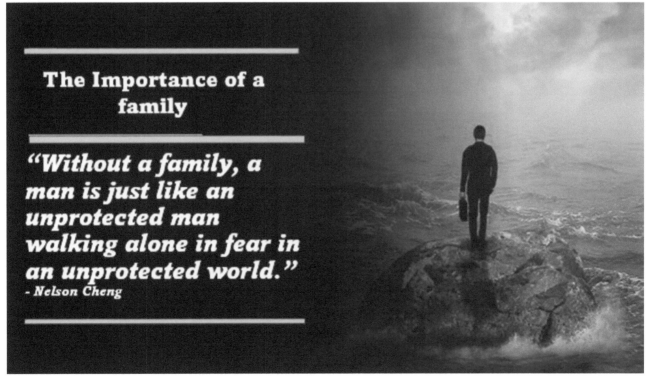

The Importance of a family

"Without a family, a man is just like an unprotected man walking alone in fear in an unprotected world."

- Nelson Cheng

Family is everything. It is not something to be taken for granted. Our fast-paced world makes it easy to forget the people who are always around us, our family members.

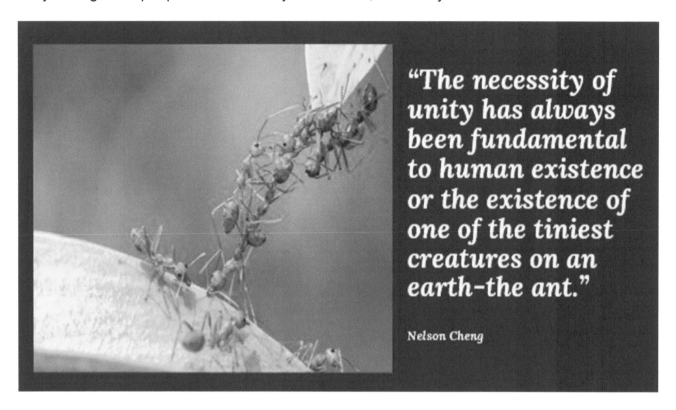

"The necessity of unity has always been fundamental to human existence or the existence of one of the tiniest creatures on an earth-the ant."

Nelson Cheng

This is even more true today as our world undergoes unprecedented changes. By embracing the spirit of unity, we will be inspired to reach out to other members of our family to maintain peace, harmony, and love within the family.

"Great things can be accomplished when we work together or when we stand together." –Nelson Cheng

The idea that we can accomplish more when we work together and stand together is well known. The same is true for the family unit. The concept of unity has been proven to have a positive impact on so many people around the world, more so in the context of a family unit.

There are instances when we overlook the importance of unity, such as forgetting to express our gratitude to family members who help us work towards our goals or not recognising the efforts or generosity of family members who improve our lives. Whenever unity is prioritised, so much can be achieved. To live a happy and successful life, it is important to promote and maintain unity in our family.

We are inspired to reach great heights by our families, and we are comforted when we falter occasionally.

"A family is like a root system. No wind is too strong when the roots are deep."
-Nelson Cheng

Families are likened to roots. When the roots are deep, there is no need to be afraid of the wind.

Trees take root deeper when they are battered by storms. Likewise, families that weathered the storms of life together will have stronger and deeper bonds.

"Families that go through adversity together will become closer."

Nelson Cheng

Families that endure adversity together will likely form stronger bonds.
—Nelson Cheng

"A closely knitted family ensures no one is forgotten or left behind." -Nelson Cheng

Strong families are those that are united, while weak families are those that are divided.
—Nelson Cheng

Someone can learn to love an imperfect you if you learn to love the imperfect member in your family.
—Nelson Cheng

The only way your family member can love you despite your imperfections is if you love them despite their shortcomings.
—Nelson Cheng

For your family member to love you despite your imperfections, you must learn to love them despite their imperfections.
—Nelson Cheng

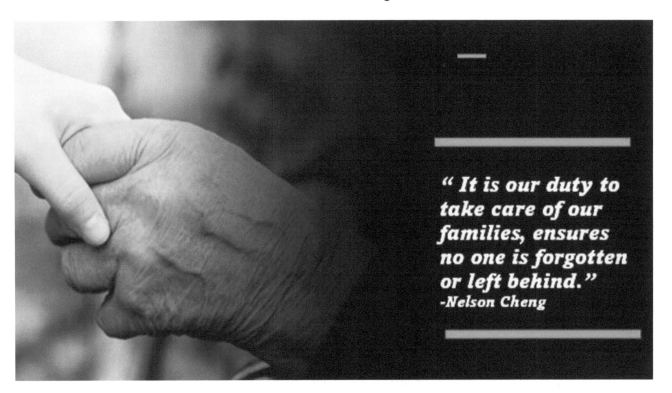

" *It is our duty to take care of our families, ensures no one is forgotten or left behind.* "
-Nelson Cheng

"*Brotherhood and sisterhood are lifelong privileges. Cherish them while you can.*"

The blessedness of togetherness as a family

Togetherness is a state of being close to our family members. We share a strong connection with the family members we are closest to during good and bad times.

When we stay united, we are provided with a sense of security, support, and inner strength, so we can overcome obstacles and achieve great things, knowing that we have the unconditional love of those around us.

Unity is strength, and it encourages us all to embrace and celebrate unity whenever we can.

It is a lifelong privilege to be a brother or sister. Cherish them while you have the chance.
—Nelson Cheng

Love perfects the imperfections.
—Nelson Cheng

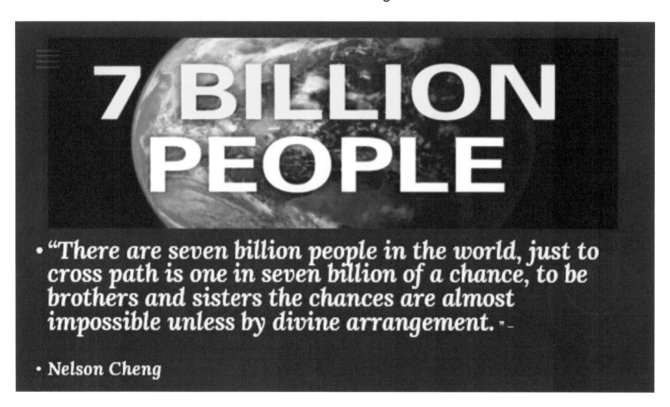

People and families intertwine and intersect in the world, creating what we call human relationships. It is through these relationships that society exists. Companionship and communication are provided by family, and love and understanding are given and received through them. Family relationships help us develop, grow, and learn, and they give us self-esteem, identity, and significance.

In addition to allowing us to give and receive love from our siblings, siblings also facilitate the development of tolerance, an appreciation for others, communication skills, forgiveness, and genuine companionship.

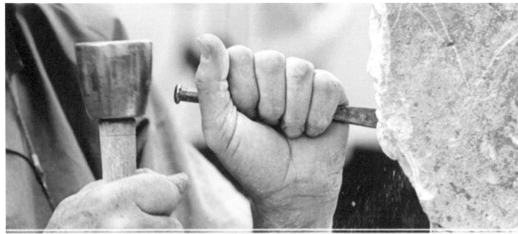

"Siblings facilitate the development of tolerance, an appreciation for others, communication skills, forgiveness, and genuine companionship." Nelson Cheng

"The power of love perfects the imperfections" Nelson Cheng

"In contrast to mere communication, communion is the most profound form of communication. The message is wordless...beyond words...beyond concepts." Nelson Cheng

As siblings, we can move from communication to communion, freely sharing our unpleasant thoughts instead of only pleasant talks.
—Nelson Cheng

A reflective poem on siblings

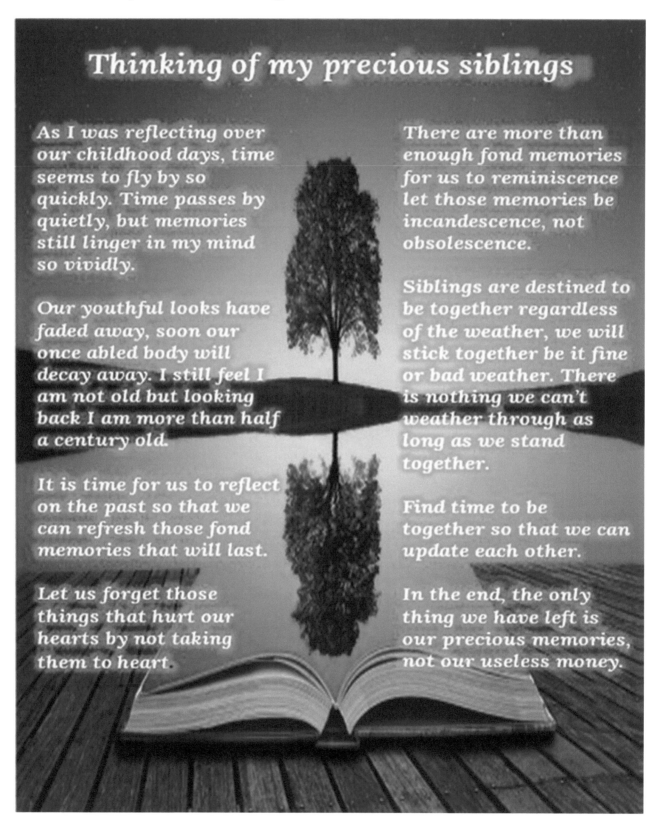

Thinking of my precious siblings

As I was reflecting over our childhood days, time seems to fly by so quickly. Time passes by quietly, but memories still linger in my mind so vividly.

Our youthful looks have faded away, soon our once abled body will decay away. I still feel I am not old but looking back I am more than half a century old.

It is time for us to reflect on the past so that we can refresh those fond memories that will last.

Let us forget those things that hurt our hearts by not taking them to heart.

There are more than enough fond memories for us to reminiscence let those memories be incandescence, not obsolescence.

Siblings are destined to be together regardless of the weather, we will stick together be it fine or bad weather. There is nothing we can't weather through as long as we stand together.

Find time to be together so that we can update each other.

In the end, the only thing we have left is our precious memories, not our useless money.

10
CHAPTER

Reflection on Simplicity of Life

"The secret to living a contented life is to live simply."

Nelson Cheng

"Nature is pleased with simplicity. And nature is no dummy"
— Isaac Newton

Why should we live simply?

Unfortunately, many people do not know how to live simply because they have adopted the philosophy of keeping up with the Joneses. Society has subtly been moulded and melded to keep up with their peers, neighbours, colleagues, etc.

With simplicity in life, we can work less on the things we dislike and more on what we love. That will allow us to spend more time with our families. Consequently, we have become more productive and have made more money because of cutting expenses.

When we live a simple lifestyle, we do more with less, we create more variety, we increase our abilities for spontaneity, we spend less time on bills, and we have more time with our families and friends.

Living simply can make our life full, happy, and fulfilling in every stage of human growth.

How would you describe living a simple life?

For some, that means a simpler life in the country, free from the bustle and noise of the city. Being at peace is the key to living a simple life for most of us. When all areas of life are balanced and tended to, a feeling of peace and contentment is likely to arise.

The essentials of living a simple life

Mindful intentions

You can truly simplify your life when you realise that a day itself composed of thousands of small, seemingly insignificant decisions that add up to your results.

The outcomes will take care of themselves when you are in control of the tiny choices you make throughout your day.

When you make decisions based on your values and mindful intentions, you should be satisfied with your results.

You will start thinking smarter instead of harder when you develop a mindset of simplicity. As you gain experience, it becomes easier to let go of the things that don't serve you.

Your routines and habits

Routine is said to be medicine. We can also think of routine and consistency as anchors that keep us from drifting into chaos.

The spontaneity of life has its place for sure. However, if you're looking for simplicity, having a routine in at least some areas of your life will keep you centred and grounded when things get rough.

Routines and habits that are established help ease 'decision fatigue'. Many of us have experienced it. There's a lot to decide about during the day: what to wear, what to eat for breakfast, how to respond to that email or text, what to make for dinner, and whether to spend money on a certain item.

It is easy to feel drained at the end of the day.

When you reach this stage, even simple decisions can seem impossible, and your ability to make good decisions has been greatly diminished.

By setting some basic behaviours and routines in place in advance, you can reduce this phenomenon to a greater extent.

Because of the small, insignificant decisions being made ahead of time, life will automatically be less stressful because more mental energy will be left for making better decisions in crucial areas.

Simplification of routines and habits allows you to focus on whatever is in front of you at any given time. By doing so, you will be more aware.

Maintaining a good health

Simple living without a particular focus on health can be challenging. When I am sick, tired, stressed, or just plain burned out . . . everything feels complicated!

A healthy lifestyle results in many benefits, including increased energy and mental clarity, making life simpler and easier to manage.

There are three simple things you can do for your health immediately that will have the biggest impact moving forward. Once these are established, you can always build upon them from there, but building these into habits is a must.

Make quality sleep a priority

Get at least seven uninterrupted hours of sleep.

One hour or more before bedtime, avoid screen time.

If you are a light sleeper, sleep at a cooler temperature and wear an eye mask and earplugs.

Diet and supplements

Start by cutting back on sugar, processed foods, and hydrogenated oils.

Increase your intake of fresh whole foods.

You should only take supplements when your diet lacks certain nutrients.

Have a comprehensive health check-up every year.

Physical activity

Maintain consistency while keeping it simple.

Do at least thirty minutes of walking or jogging each day.

You should always train your cardiovascular system, your muscular system, and your flexibility.

By prioritising these factors, you will notice an improvement in your overall health, energy level, and stress levels. Certain ease and simplicity will return to your life.

Positive relationships

Health is also closely related to this key.

Life is simpler and easier to bear when we have people whom we can turn to, rely on, and reach out to for support. The relationship will feel rich, full, and effortless when we feel heard and understood.

Interpersonal relationships are built on communication. Our lives will be easier if we are able to communicate effectively with all the people in our lives.

One of the best-known ways to become a master communicator is to practice non-violent communication. This practice assumes that we all have empathy and compassion within us.

Conversely, most people resort to yelling or harmful behaviour only when they see no other option for voicing their opinions.

The goal of non-violent communication is to promote understanding and empathetic listening to the other person.

There are three main objectives: supporting individual change, supporting interpersonal change, and supporting group and social changes.

Relationships become simpler; life becomes lighter when communication is effective.

Organising space and reducing clutter

Noise and clutter from outside should not invade your home. Living spaces should inspire simplicity and relaxation.

Our approach to space and clutter is to organise what you already have before you even consider decluttering.

By organising your home, you get a clear picture of what you already own, and you can make sure that each item has a designated spot where it can be easily accessed and stored.

Then you can see what might be missing, what might be damaged, or what might be duplicated. Having a place for everything makes it easier to toss out (and replace) items as necessary.

Focus on quality rather than quantity

Think about organising and labelling rather than throwing it away immediately.

With that part taken care of, you can choose wisely what stays and what needs to go. It gives you the opportunity to be intentional and choose the things you really want.

Plan your time and schedule

Time is the essence of life. We'll be on track to achieving that simple, meaningful life we're pursuing when we ensure our time is spent with intention.

How can you simplify your time and schedule?

Start with your priorities

Prioritising categorising is what we call it. To be intentional is the key. Make sure your values match your priorities and set your schedule accordingly.

Being aware of where time is being wasted is an easy way to reclaim 'lost time'.

Do you find yourself scrolling mindlessly on your phone?

Are you losing hours to your favourite show?

Do you spend hours in the store when time-saving services are available and you could be at home with your family?

It is important to become aware of the time and take action to address it, no matter what it is. You should make the necessary adjustments wherever you feel that time is taking you away from your most important priorities.

Budgets

Living a simple life with little money isn't what we're after.

Simple living would be impossible if you were worried about paying the bills and saving for the future. Budgeting doesn't need to be difficult. Your plans will be more likely to be implemented if they're simple.

To simplify your finances, we only need to focus on three areas: banking, budgeting, and investing.

Banking

You can think of your bank as the foundation of your finances since it's where you deposit and withdraw money. The bank we use has no fees of any kind, is a modern app, and allows instant money transfers.

You can also set up recurring bills with the bank. If you use products and services regularly, you can automate as many of your bills as you can.

Budgeting

Next, you should focus on your budget. Simplicity is key. While everyone's situation differs, here are some good guidelines: invest 10 per cent of your income (after building an emergency fund) and 20 per cent to pay off your debt (or save for big purchases); 70 per cent for your living expenses.

If you ignore any of those three categories completely, you will stunt your financial growth.

Investments

No matter what the economy and the markets are doing, we believe that investments should be both safe and profitable.

The Permanent Portfolio has been used by our organisation for many years now, and we are pleased with the results and simplicity. Safety is prioritised, while the upside potential is not sacrificed too much.

A simple life is a path to peace. Living simply requires balance.

Bringing mindfulness and intentional attention to each area of life will result in simplicity.

Chaos results when one is not mindful. Being mindful results in simplicity.

11

CHAPTER

Reflection on Health

Reflection on Health

"We are made up of the body, soul, and spirit, hence, we are not truly healthy until we are wholesome in these three faculties."
– Nelson Cheng

"Some people are funny when they were young, they made wealth at the expense of their health and when they grow old, they will spend all their wealth to regain their health."

Nelson Cheng

What is health?

A healthy state is an overall state of good physical, mental, and spiritual well-being, which involves following daily advice and taking preventive measures to limit the possibility of diseases.

Physical health

Health describes the body's ability to perform fundamental functions such as breathing, moving, and digesting, as well as adapting to the physical, psychological, and social changes it faces.

It also refers to the protection of the body against physical, social, and mental disorders.

Mental health

A person's mental health determines whether they can perform their everyday life tasks correctly. It means that a person's body does not contain any diseases in all parts of his body and all its internal organs are intact.

While social health is represented by the ability of a person to accomplish social tasks entrusted to him without defect or error.

Spiritual health

We can contribute to healing through our spiritual lives. We can cope with pain and difficulties accompanied by illness with the help of spirituality. The goal of spiritual health is to feel at peace with life. We can find hope and comfort during even the darkest of times. This can be a great support as you live your life to the fullest. Spiritual health is important to the wholesomeness of our well-being.

Why health is the most important part of your life

Physical health

It is essential to be healthy if you want to feel happy, as there are many people who suffer from diseases, but being healthy allows them to fight their ailments and achieve fitness. Ultimately, they feel comfortable and enjoy life like any other person.

Life revolves around your health. Good health is essential to all aspects of your life. If you are in poor health, then you cannot reach your full potential.

Having ill health may make you look inward rather than outward at helping others. You will not be able to support your parents and family appropriately, have fun with friends if you are lethargic and dull, and you will not be able to learn and grow if your body is weak. Health is the foundation of everything!

Healthy people are those who can serve themselves, their nation, and their communities.

Those who are unhealthy suffer from weakness and meagreness, unable to effectively perform their duties and responsibilities.

The person becomes dependent on other people and unable to meet his different needs, causing him to feel helpless and weak. This affects his psychological state as well. Furthermore, society suffers because of the presence of the disease among its members, since the productivity of these patients declines, and they become dependent on society.

The presence of healthy individuals in society is defined by the presence of productive individuals who can give and serve.

Mental health

People who are mentally healthy feel comfortable and happy in their lives and are well able to enjoy life.

Mentally ill individuals always appear gloomy and pessimistic to others and do not feel happy in their lives or relationships.

A healthy person shows love, kindness, and intimacy towards others and enjoys happiness in one's life.

Spiritual health

Finally, we should consider our spiritual health in life to avoid diseases that disrupt our lives and realise that illness may just be one of the many trials we face in our lives.

Having a chronic illness may cause you to lose your spirituality. It is possible to become tempted to abandon your beliefs at times. It is important to remember that your physical health can be improved by maintaining a healthy spiritual life. Physical health issues can be dealt with through your spiritual life. We are holistic beings. Our spiritual well-being depends on maintaining a sense of balance.

"The three aspects of our life–the physical, mental, and spiritual–influence each other in a symbiotic way."
Nelson Cheng

As human beings, we are holistic. We need a sense of balance to be physically, mentally, and spiritually well.
—Nelson Cheng

The three aspects of our life—the physical, and mental, and spiritual—influence each other in a symbiotic way. People are often unaware that our health relates to these three aspects of our life in a symbiotic way.

12
CHAPTER

Reflection on How to Achieve Good Health and Well-Being

Eat healthily

Your health is closely linked to what you eat. You can boost your immune system, maintain a healthy weight, and improve your overall health by eating a healthy diet.

Eat more fruits and vegetables

Make sure to include fruits, vegetables, grains, leafy greens, salmon, etc. as part of your diet. Adding fruits and vegetables to your diet is an ideal way to start a healthy routine.

Stay hydrated

When you drink lots of water, you keep your muscles and joints working, you increase the amount of water in your blood, you promote healthy skin and cardiovascular health, and you cleanse your body of toxins.

By drinking water throughout the day, you can save a lot of money and improve your health at the same time.

Exercise regularly

It is important that you engage in moderate exercise for at least thirty minutes a day, since exercise can help prevent heart disease, stroke, colon cancer, and diabetes.

Reduce your weight

If you are overweight, you should lose weight. You have to decrease your calorie consumption if you want to lose extra weight, so you will have to start keeping track of what you eat.

You can reduce the risk of heart disease, cancer, and diabetes by losing weight if you are obese.

Protect your skin

The skin is the first line of defence in the body, and it needs to be protected at all costs. It can be very harmful to your skin cells during the summer months since a lot of sun exposure will cause your skin cells to be damaged or even destroyed by UV rays.

Winter is a time when most of us are plagued by fluctuations, redness, allergies, and irritation of the skin.

As a result of cold temperatures and low humidity levels, dry air is created, which pulls moisture away from the skin. Therefore, you need to always protect your skin.

Make sure that you get enough sleep every night

Sleep plays an important role in your overall health and well-being because it allows your body to repair itself and makes you fit and ready for the day ahead.

You may be able to prevent physical health problems such as excessive weight gain and heart disease if you get enough sleep at the right time. It can also help you to keep your mental health in check, improve your quality of life, and help you stay safe.

Avoid substance abuse

It is important to stay away from tobacco, alcohol, caffeine, and sugary drinks. As much as possible, avoid smoking, drinking alcohol, and consuming tobacco since they will harm your health in the long run.

When you stop smoking, you will greatly reduce your risk of dying from lung cancer and other potentially life-threatening diseases such as heart disease, stroke, emphysema, chronic bronchitis, etc.

Improve your lifestyle

If you want to live a healthy, happy life, then you will understand what to do. Poor lifestyle is a significant contributor to the development and progression of chronic diseases, which are preventable.

Make healthy lifestyle choices, adopt good dietary habits, and adopt a healthy lifestyle design so that you can make positive changes in your life.

Get some exercise and find ways to reduce your stress and depression by making time to exercise.

Your energy levels reflect your overall health and well-being. It is true that if you have more energy throughout the day, you will be able to achieve a lot more than you would without it. Considering that every day is the same length, the difference between us can only be the amount of energy we bring to each of the aspects of our lives.

Often, people are not aware that health is interconnected with the other aspects of life in a symbiotic manner. The health of an individual is composed of four layers of energy: physical, mental, emotional, and spiritual.

A great deal of attention is devoted to the physical layer. Deeper and more powerful layers of the mind, emotions, and spirituality are responsible for determining your energy, appetite, liveliness, passion, as well as your feelings in general. There are many people who feel low energy, general unhappiness, anxiety, and unfulfilled no matter how healthy they eat, how they exercise, and how they meditate. What's wrong with that?

The four energies of your life must be aligned for high sustainable energy. In what ways can they be aligned? You can align them by living consciously in each of the seven areas. Living a full, complete, and fulfilling life in all seven areas is where your true source of energy comes from.

Your life force will shine brightly when you live consciously in each of these seven aspects. Every time one aspect of life is neglected, your life force dims. As you neglect more, the dimming continues. Neglect them all, and you will lose energy. Many people view anxiety and depression as nothing more than a sign that they have stopped climbing higher and started neglecting their loved ones, families, friendships, a sense of contribution and charity, and continued learning.

Mental, emotional, and spiritual health are affected by these parts of yourself. Physical health is a product of these parts of yourself. Therefore, being healthy is more than just eating right, exercising, and sleeping well.

Most people are unaware of how to live a conscious life in each of this area. The information is too overwhelming, and there is no framework for living consciously.

13
CHAPTER

Reflection on Discipline

What is discipline?

Generally, discipline is characterised by a set of actions or rules that are applied to regulate the behaviour of humans in the society or environment to which they belong.

A person's discipline is a set of rules that allows them to live their lives in a more efficient and effective manner. With a certain degree of discipline in your life, you can make small sacrifices in your present for the future satisfaction of your life. Discipline creates habits, habits make routines, and routines become who you are daily.

How do develop discipline?

Discipline is like a muscle that can be developed. Through consistent practice, discipline becomes stronger. In sports, it is common to see the disciplined team defeat the less disciplined team with better talent. Team members who are disciplined can see the big picture and use restraint in the face of adversity. If the team is not as disciplined, they end up losing their cool and they end up blowing their chance. It is a discipline that has been developed through hours of training, holding one another accountable, and doing things that others are not prepared to do.

How does discipline lead to success?

I believe that the key to success in life is self-discipline. Without it, it is impossible to succeed in life. Those who are successful will always advise you to remain disciplined in your life.

However, the question remains: Why is self-discipline important for success in the long run? Self-discipline is one of the most important factors that will help you become an unstoppable force of energy to reach the greatest level in your life.

It is a self-discipline that helps us to overcome laziness and procrastination and prevents us from taking things for granted when they are given to us. Those who are self-disciplined take control of their lives.

It is through self-discipline that habits are formed. You can make or break your life based on your habits. Self-discipline creates a habit in your life that can only be built up by committing to it.

Laziness is the main reason why a lot of people are unable to remain disciplined in their lives. On the other hand, laziness is also a habit that needs to be overcome. People who accomplish success discipline themselves to work and stay consistent with it. As a result, it becomes a habit. As a result, they can attract success in their lives.

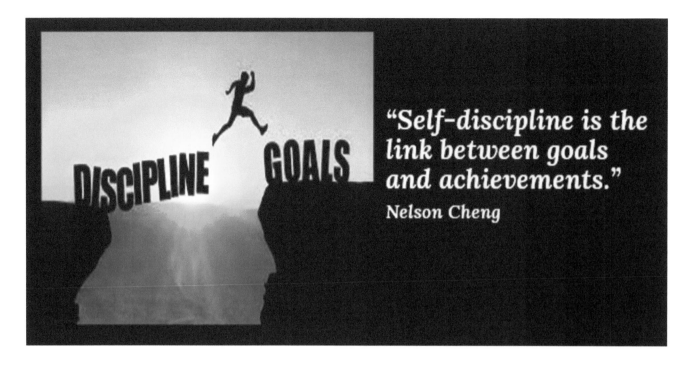

With discipline, you learn to take control of your mind, feelings, and actions to stay on track until you accomplish what you set out to do.

It is important to realise that discipline isn't just about abstinence, controlling reactions, getting up early, and working till late at night. This is but one aspect of what discipline is. In addition to giving you control and mastery over your life and your actions, discipline gives you energy, willpower, motivation, and inner strength.

Discipline provides you with the ability to cope calmly with difficult situations, and the perseverance and persistence to continue with your actions, despite challenges.

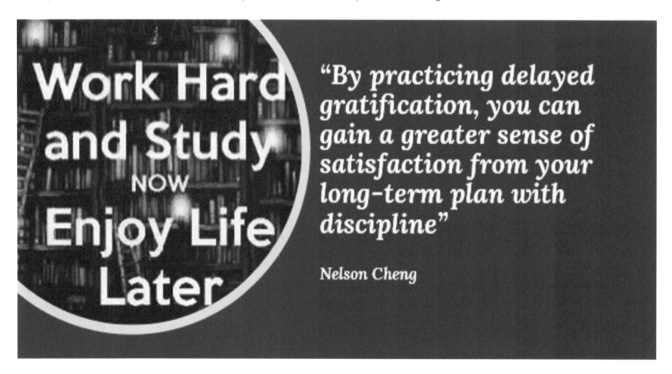

It is certain that those who can delay gratification in the short term to enjoy greater rewards in the long term are sure to succeed. One of the best examples of this is Michael Phelps.

The most decorated Olympian of all time, Michael Phelps discusses his and his coach Bob Bowman's approach in the book No Limits. A habit they have is doing things that unsuccessful people do not like to do. There is no shortage of talented individuals. However, Bowman and Phelps are willing to go further, work harder, and be more committed and dedicated than anyone else.

Between 1998 and 2003, they did not believe in days off. The first came because of a snowstorm, and the second and third were because of wisdom teeth extraction. He has missed three days in five years. During that period, he missed only three days out of a total of 1,825 days. The discipline he has shown is the reason for the twenty-eight Olympic medals he has won, twenty-three of which are gold.

There is no doubt that self-discipline is one of the most important characteristics of becoming successful. Staying focused on your goals will give you the mental fortitude needed to persevere with difficult tasks, and, more importantly, you will be able to embrace obstacles and discomfort as you push yourself to new heights.

Self-discipline is one of the cornerstones of success.
—Nelson Cheng

To achieve success, self-discipline is one of the most important components.

14
CHAPTER

Reflection on Hard Work

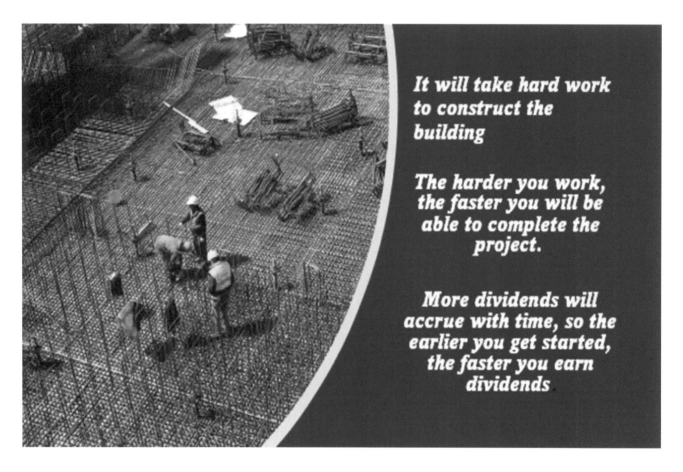

It will take hard work to construct the building

The harder you work, the faster you will be able to complete the project.

More dividends will accrue with time, so the earlier you get started, the faster you earn dividends.

As with interest, hard work compounds with time, so the earlier you start, the quicker you get your dividends.
—Nelson Cheng

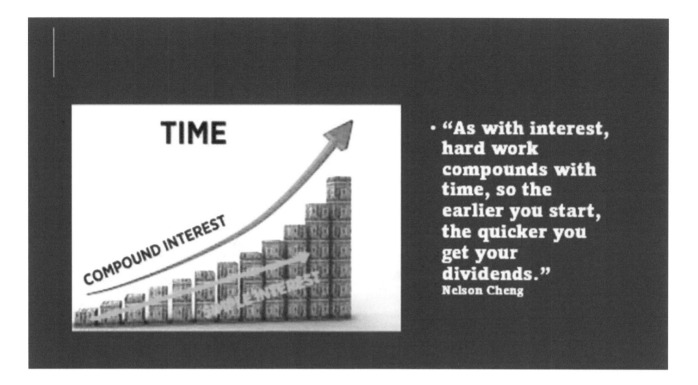

The importance and benefits of hard work

It improves our livelihood.

A challenge and growth opportunity are inherent in hard work. When we work hard, our skills and abilities improve; and as we do, we become better versions of ourselves. As we grow, we will become better at work, and we will be able to improve our livelihood to a greater extent.

Hard work brings benefits to society.

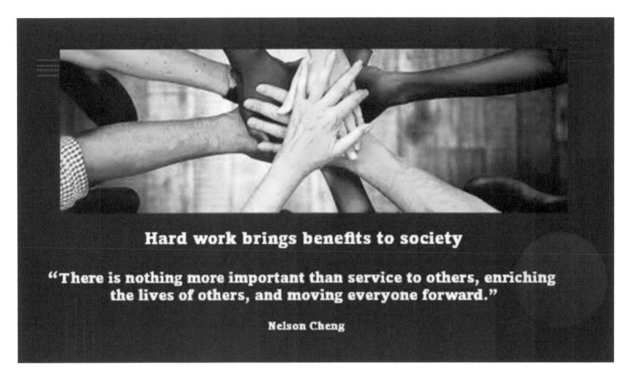

Hard work brings benefits to society

"There is nothing more important than service to others, enriching the lives of others, and moving everyone forward."

Nelson Cheng

The hard work we do contributes to the good of society. There is nothing more important than being of service to others, enriching the lives of others, and moving everyone forward. I guess you could say that as give our services, be it solving corrosion problems, curing cancer, or serving at the restaurant, our hard work can be viewed as an act of love to those we serve.

Hard work is an example our children should follow.

Hard work is an example our children should follow.

• *"As a parent, one of the most important values that I hope to pass on to my children is the importance of working hard on the things that matter."*

• Nelson Cheng

86

The more effort we put into achieving our best work each day, the more our kids will take notice. As a parent, one of the most important values that I hope to pass on to my children is the importance of working hard on the things that matter.

The lessons of life are learned.

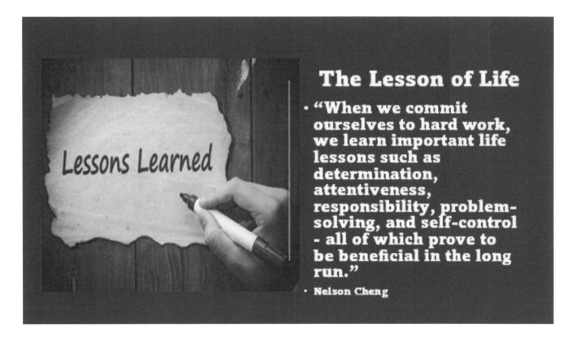

When we commit ourselves to hard work, we learn important life lessons such as determination, attentiveness, responsibility, problem-solving, and self-control—all of which prove to be beneficial in the long run. By doing so, we can learn from these lessons and apply them elsewhere (health, relationships, hobbies, etc.).

Make the most of the time that you have at your disposal.

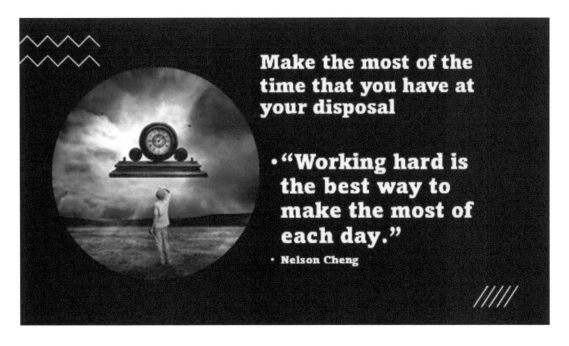

Whenever a new day dawns, we are faced with a choice: fill this day with the best of what we have or let it slip away. We have no choice; the hours will pass regardless of what we do. Working hard is the best way to make the most of each day.

It is rewarding to work.

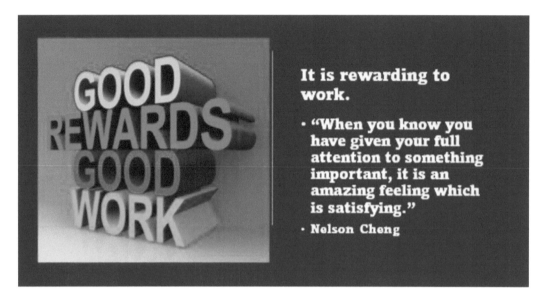

As far as I'm concerned, there are fewer joys in life more satisfying than lying down at night with tired legs attached to a tired body, especially after a long day. When you know you have given your full attention to something important, it is an amazing feeling, which is satisfying.

We stay occupied with important issues by working hard.

There are several dangers associated with living a life of inactivity. It helps keep us from making selfish and foolish decisions with idle time when we choose to use our time and energy on things that will bring value to others and not ourselves.

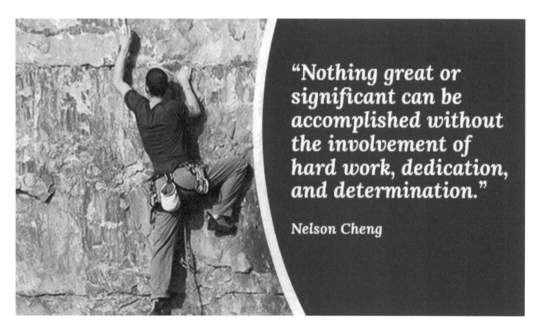

15
CHAPTER

Reflection on Self-Improvement

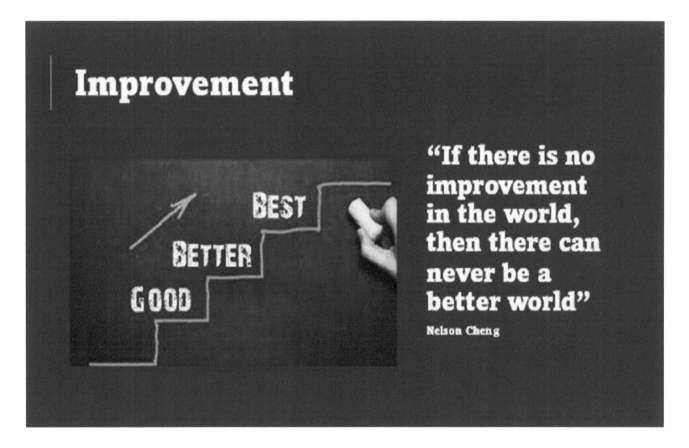

If there is no improvement in the world, then there can never be a better world. It is for that reason that we each must work for our own improvement as well as share a general responsibility for all of humankind. Our duty is to assist those to whom we think we can be of most use.

Kaizen

In Japan, the practice of continuous process improvement (also known as kaizen) was developed to reduce the costs associated with the manufacturing process and improve its quality. *Kaizen* is a Japanese term that means 'change for better', a simple concept that today is being used not just by individuals but also by teams and organisations all over the world.

The importance of self-improvement

Our parents taught us, since we were young, the importance of mastering academics, the importance of getting good grades, and the importance of acing our exams. Traditionally, school and college learning has always been primarily focused on academic courses, but what about aspects such as self-improvement and personal development, which are equally important for people's lives as academic courses?

There is a tendency for self-improvement to go unnoticed despite its importance. It's convenient to brush our shortcomings under the carpet; either we're refusing to confront them or we're just happy to be ignorant. It's not possible to run away from your own shortcomings. It has been said that the farther you run, the deeper a grave you dig because there will come a time when all your unresolved feelings will surface, leaving you feeling overwhelmed.

Then, what is the best thing that you can do? Make the decision to improve yourself an integral part of your life by consciously becoming more self-aware, observing your thoughts, emotions, and reactions, and then committing to self-improvement.

It is important not to stop learning just as it is important to never stop improving oneself. As a matter of fact, the idea that we should focus on continuous self-development at every stage of our lives and strive to become better versions of ourselves should be the focus.

How to develop for self-improvement irrespective of age

Develop a greater sense of self-awareness

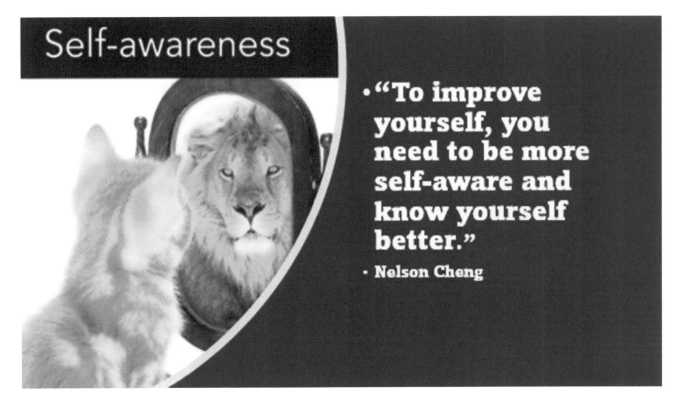

Self-awareness

• "To improve yourself, you need to be more self-aware and know yourself better."
- Nelson Cheng

In our company, we spend a lot of time getting to know our customers and solving their problems. The world would have been so much different if only we had spent that much time studying ourselves.

To improve yourself, you need to be more self-aware and know yourself better. The experience makes you question yourself and face reality for what it is, regardless of how harsh it may seem.

Self-awareness is an ongoing process—as you go through life, you are met with new experiences and challenges that allow you to become more aware of your personality, thoughts, and feelings. As a result, to remain on the path of self-improvement, it is important never to lose sight of who you are.

Strengthen your strengths

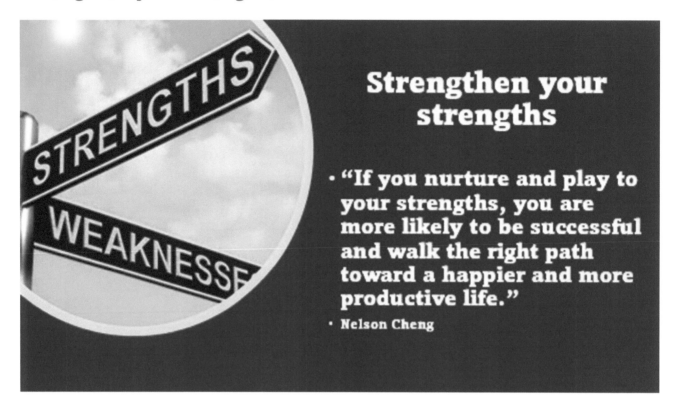

As a result of self-improvement, you are able to identify your personal strengths and make the most of them. You need to know your strengths in every aspect of your life, from relationships to career, to be successful.

This allows you to gain a better sense of what you are seeking as well as where you are likely to thrive and excel. Setting life goals and doing what you must do are important parts of the process. In the end, you can only accomplish what you want when you know exactly what you want.

If you nurture and play to your strengths, you are more likely to be successful and walk the right path towards a happier and more productive life.

Be aware of your weaknesses and overcome them

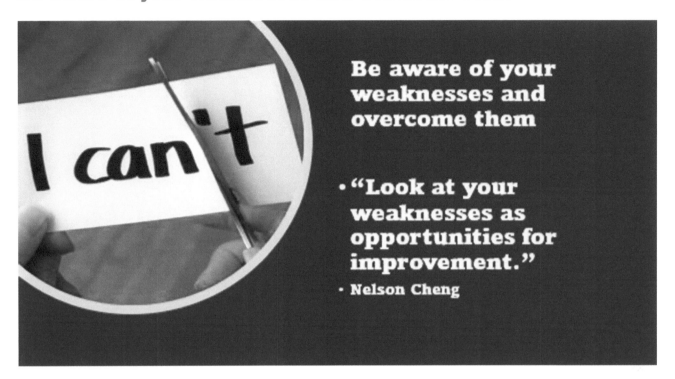

As important as it is to identify your strengths, it is also important that you become aware of your weaknesses as part of your self-improvement process. Look at them as opportunities to improve. Each of us has strengths and weaknesses. This is what makes us human.

Improve yourself by looking beyond those weaknesses that stop you from being great. Be aware of your weaknesses, identify where they originate, and overcome them.

The task is not easy, but it is certainly not impossible. Make sure every weakness you have becomes a strength as you continue your journey of self-improvement.

Don't stay in your comfort zone

There is a danger in staying in your comfort zone for too long. Even though it is nice to feel good about something, it also denotes stagnancy, and stagnancy is not conducive to growth.

You need to step out of your comfort zone if you are going to work on improving yourself. By trying new things, taking risks, and challenging yourself, you are forced to face your fears. In between times when you will succeed and times when you will fail, there will also be times when you will discover a new side of yourself.

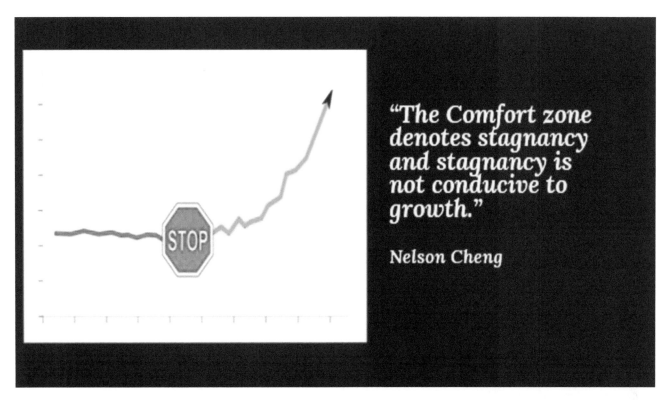

"The Comfort zone denotes stagnancy and stagnancy is not conducive to growth."

Nelson Cheng

"Self-improvement is a process that is never completed".

Nelson Cheng

16
CHAPTER

Reflection on the Word of God

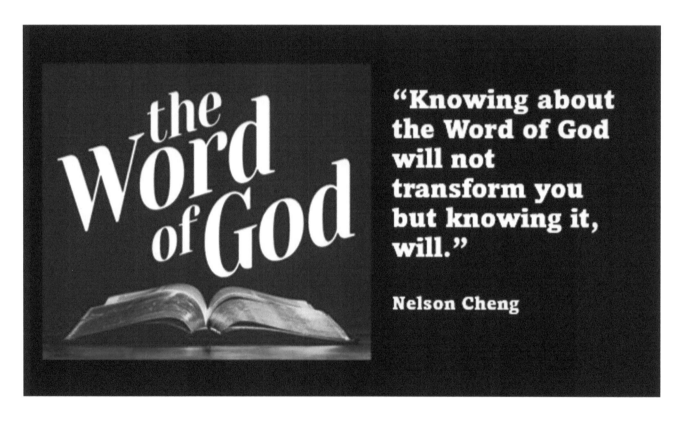

the Word of God

"Knowing about the Word of God will not transform you but knowing it, will."

Nelson Cheng

The importance of knowing the Word of God

Do you know Jesus as the true Word, who gives light and life?

In the beginning was the Word, and the Word was with God, and the Word was God.
—John 1:1

There is no God of coincidences or chaos, and Jesus wasn't one. The words of John show that Jesus was God in the beginning. His life on this earth was part of a plan that began from the beginning, since He is God, one with God.

What was 'the Word'? (And how was it 'with God'?)

God spoke the world into existence. 'Let there be light' was his first command (Gen. 1:3). It separated the light from the darkness.

The Greek word for 'word' is *logos*, which means 'a message, a report, or a word'. According to John, this logos was in the beginning, was with God all the time, and was God himself.

John 1:1 mentions God as omnipotent and sovereign. All things are held together by the Word, Logos, and Jesus Christ. Christ is the fulfilment of God's covenant with his people. 'He is before all things, and in Him, all things hold together' (Col. 1:17).

Knowing God's Word is to know God himself.
—Nelson Cheng

Knowing about the Word of God is one thing but knowing the Word of God is another. The difference is in personal relationships. The fact that God is a person means that you can learn about him without really knowing him until you have a personal relationship with him.

As an example, I can know about Mr Lee Hsieh Loong, the prime minister of Singapore, but I would not say that I know him. To know him, I need to meet him and get to know him. I think that we must open up to one another and be willing to share the things in our lives with each other. I am in awe at the promise of the Bible that we can know God just like that and that he wants us to know him and be a part of his eternal life!

It is possible to know God as a person. If God is a person, how would we know that? The Lord came down to earth in the person of Jesus Christ and made himself a man. The reason Jesus came to earth was not just to heal them and teach them how to become better people. He was primarily sent to reveal who (not 'what') God is and how we can have a relationship with him. Even though God is one eternal being, he exists in the relationship of three different persons: Father, Son, and Spirit.

The benefit of knowing God's Word

In the chaotic world we live in, where everything continues to change or evolve at an unprecedented rate in human history, we must rely on the wisdom of God to make the right choice or decision in our careers, businesses, education, relationships, etc.

There's no better place to look for guidance than the Word of God.

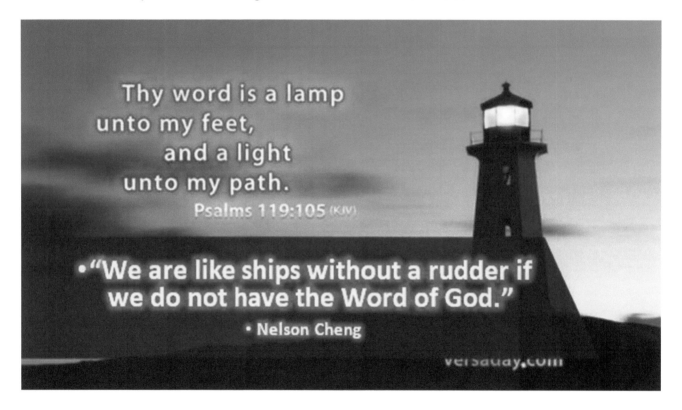

Thy word is a lamp
unto my feet,
and a light
unto my path.
Psalms 119:105 (KJV)

• "We are like ships without a rudder if we do not have the Word of God."
• Nelson Cheng

As a lamp that lights our way

The Word of God has been compared to a lamp that lights our way and a lamp that lights our feet. It guides us in the dark stormy weather, it guides us in our work, and it guides us in our way. We would indeed be in a dark place without it. The commandments of God are like a lamp kept burning with the oil of the Holy Spirit as a light to guide us in taking the path we choose and the steps we take along the way.

The word of God is like a torch or lamp to a man on a dark night. It shows him the way; it prevents him from stumbling over obstacles, falling down precipices, or wandering off into paths that would lead to danger, or turns him away altogether from the path to life with all doubts and difficulties, and comforts him in his fears and distresses.

> *In the chaotic world, we live in, where everything continues to change or evolve at an unprecedented rate in human history, we must rely on the wisdom of God to make the right choice or decision in our careers, businesses, education, relationships, etc.*
> —Nelson Cheng

God's Word is a compass

Sometimes, I feel lost in this overwhelming world when I wonder what the next step should be. I don't know about you, but I need help getting back on track. I need a compass to lead me in the right direction. That compass is God's Word.

It provides guidance and direction to our lives. There is an arrow pointing in the direction in which one should travel. There is no better instrument that I can use to lead me to what is right and what is true than the word of God.

Mariners need precise measurements. There's no room for intuition or memory. They need a compass to get that accurate reading, especially when surrounded by water.

To guide me towards God's plan for my life, I need to rely on His Word as my most accurate guide. His Word provides me with not only hope and encouragement but also the most accurate measurements to help me choose the right course when I am lost in a sea of hurt or trouble. His

Word leads me out of the darkness when I am engulfed in it. 'Your word is a lamp for my feet, a light on my path,' Psalm 119:105 says.

You need to lay down a compass on a level surface. Compass needles are inaccurate when used on a tilt. God's Word must be applied correctly. I must not miss the context before and after a verse to be accurately pointed in the right direction. These contexts provide the actual direction and instructions. The truth and the way are revealed in their entirety and lead me down the right path with hope. Romans 15:4, says, 'For everything written in the past was written to teach us so that through the endurance taught in the Scriptures and the encouragement provided by them we might have hope.'

You and I have been given this compass, the Word of God. It gives us a true understanding of the goodness that God provides. The Word lays out the path to salvation and righteous life for us. Knowing I can depend on the compass as I navigate this life gives me peace and hope. May the word of God also be your compass.

There is no better instrument that I can use to lead me to what is right and what is true than the word of God.
—Nelson Cheng

The Word of God is just like a rudder of a ship; it directs us in the right direction to subjugate the storms of life.

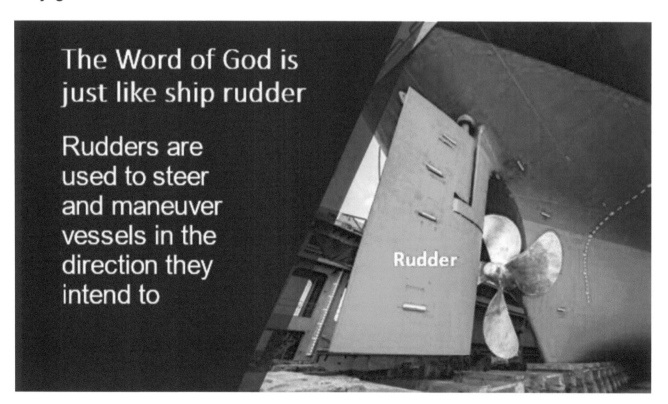

Oh, and ships! They are terribly large and are driven along by very strong winds, yet they are guided by a very small rudder wherever the will of the helmsman directs.
—James 3:4

It is a marvel of human ingenuity that man can subjugate two forces that appear so wild and untameable, the wind and the sea, to use for his benefit. This is not human arrogance, but human genius coupled with obedience to God's command: 'Fill the world and subdue it' (Gen. 1:28). By building a vessel large enough, its keel and rudder can 'bite' into the tide or current, offset by using stretched canvas sails that catch the wind and propel the vessel forward even when the wind isn't blowing in the right direction. No matter whether sails are used, it is the rudder under the water that turns the whole vessel.

The Word of God is just like a rudder of a ship; it directs us in the right direction to subjugate the storms of life.
—Nelson Cheng

God's Word provides direction

We all need God's guidance to direct our decisions in life. Proverbs 3:5–6 (NIV) says, 'Trust in the LORD with all your heart and lean not on your own understanding; in all your ways acknowledge him, and he will make your paths straight.' In these verses, God's Word warns us not to rely on our own understanding.

We trust God because we know he is always in control of whatever happens in our lives. He does everything for our own good, even when we don't understand.

When everything is going according to plan, it is easy to believe in God. The real test is when everything starts to break down. Do we still have faith in God when we don't understand things?

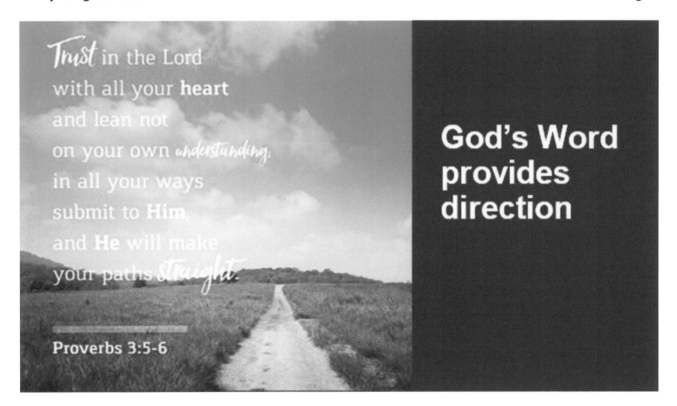

101

When you don't know what lies ahead, it can be hard to trust God. However, if you trust God, once you're out of the darkness and into the light, you can look back and gain a better understanding. You will soon understand why things happened the way they did, and everything will suddenly make sense.

It is a comfort to know that if we trust God, he will work all things together for the good of those who love him, to those who are called according to his purpose (Rom. 8:28).

17

CHAPTER

Reflection on Reinventing the Wheel

Don't reinvent the wheel, just tweak It to suit your needs

Wheels are one of humanity's greatest inventions since they help reduce friction between objects on the surface (ground), allowing us to move objects efficiently from one place to another, and eventually laying the foundation for further inventions.

What does reinventing mean?

Despite its age, the idiom 'reinventing the wheel' may not be as old as you think it is. Reinventing the wheel means trying to create something that has already been created by someone else or solving a problem that has already been solved. In this idiom, the wheel is referred to as an invention that already exists, so wasting time and resources on a solved problem is inexcusable. It is often used as a warning against wasting time and effort in any industry, where the employee should not waste time on common problems previously solved by their predecessors or other people.

The act of reinventing the wheel refers to reproducing a method that has already been created or optimised by others, wasting invaluable time and resources on a solved problem is inexcusable.
—Nelson Cheng

Do you need to reinvent the wheel?

An attempt to reinvent it would be pointless, would add no value to the original object, and would divert the investigator's time and effort from possibly more useful endeavours. Given it has been invented and is not considered to have any flaws operationally, attempts to reinvent it would be pointless and useless.

What are the negative effects of reinventing the wheel?

It is negative to try to reinvent the wheel—for example, coming up with something that has been known for a long time and is common knowledge and presenting it as if it were something innovative and new, or putting a lot of work and research into coming up with a well-known result is simply a waste of time, effort, and resources.

Isn't it better to borrow ideas and improve on them than reinvent the wheel?

"SMART AND RESOURCEFUL PERSON BORROWS IDEAS AND IMPROVES THEM RATHER THAN REINVENTING THE WHEEL REPEATEDLY."
NELSON CHENG

Borrowing ideas and improving on them

SOLDIERS CLEANING THE GUN BARREL OF THE MAIN BATTLE TANK USING POLES AND BORE BRUSH

In seeing soldiers using a long pole and bore brush to clean a howitzer gun barrel, I thought how I could help by simply using their bore brush with an automatic winch.

The borrowed idea of cleaning the gun barrel ultimately led to the invention of the Vappro ABC-Automatic Barrel Cleaner.

The invention of the Vappro Automatic Barrel Cleaner was a borrowed idea from the conventional pole and bore brush barrel cleaning-kit

Smart and resourceful person borrows ideas and improves them rather than reinventing the wheel repeatedly.
—Nelson Cheng

18

CHAPTER

Reflection on Failure

Society tends to celebrate success over the epic journeys to success, which are filled with trials, tribulations, setbacks, and failures. Those things are not as glamorous to talk about. Failure is an inevitable part of life, which is why this is the longest chapter of the book. If you fail at any point, I urge all readers not to give up.

If you don't quit, you haven't failed. With a positive attitude, failure is just a lesson that will prepare you to try again after getting your thoughts in order.
—Nelson Cheng

It is essential that we understand the important lesson of failure.

As an entrepreneur and a researcher, I failed numerous times in business approaches and experiments, but I kept trying and learned from my failures, leading me to become one of Singapore's leading entrepreneurs and inventors.

No matter how painful a failure may be, it is imperative to learn from it. We are all bound to fail at some point in our lives. Although I have failed numerous times, each failure has been a learning experience for me. Every time I fail, I learn something new, and each failure serves as a steppingstone towards success.

There is no greater teacher in life than failure.

If you're anything like me, then you've also probably failed multiple times; but with its life-altering lessons, it does make me a better person.

As a matter of fact, failure is life's greatest teacher. Even though failing may disappoint me in a small way, it will not cause me to give up a worthwhile endeavour. It is nature's chisel that chips away at all the excess and transforms us into the person God intended us to be. If we didn't fail, we wouldn't be capable of empathy, compassion, kindness, or achieving great things.

Whenever we think of failure, we see things in a negative light. Failure hurts, it causes emotional turmoil and upset, and it inflicts agonising feelings of guilt, regret, and remorse. Yet for those who have experienced true failure and have rebounded from it, failure in life is essential to achieving success.

Those who are most successful in life have failed the most times. Life isn't really life if you don't fail at anything at all. We become who we are by trying again and again despite failures.

Lessons from Lincoln's failures

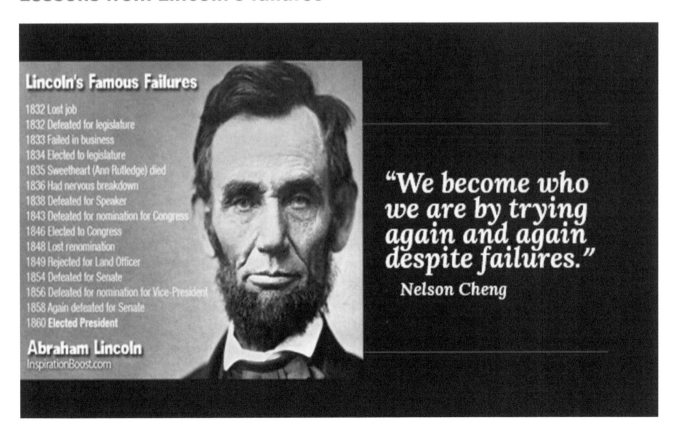

107

We become who we are by trying again and again despite failures.
— Nelson Cheng

The life of Abraham Lincoln before his presidency

A humble one-room log cabin with dirt floors in Hardin County, Kentucky, was Lincoln's birthplace. Lincoln's father, Thomas Lincoln, couldn't read or write. Abraham did not like his stern nature very much. Thomas Lincoln, whose parents were impoverished, moved his family from Kentucky to Indiana when Abraham Lincoln was seven years old. Thomas, his wife, Abraham, and elder daughter, Sarah, lived in a 360-square-foot log cabin built by Thomas.

As a nine-year-old, Lincoln lost his mother, Nancy Hanks. He rarely mentioned her in his conversations or writings, despite his later assertion that he owed everything to her guidance. Following Nancy's death, Thomas Lincoln married Sarah Bush Johnston, and Abe quickly bonded with his stepmother. In addition to encouraging Abe's education, she took his side in the frequent fights he had with his father.

Frontier life in early 1800s America was difficult. Young Abraham's life was dominated by poverty, farm chores, hard work, and reading by the light of the fireplace until he was seventeen when he found work on a ferryboat. Two years later, he built a flatboat and ran a load of farm produce down the Mississippi River to New Orleans. When he returned home, he sold the boat for its timber. When he reached home, he gave his father his full earnings resentfully but dutifully.

After Abe turned twenty-one, the family moved again, this time to Illinois, just west of Decatur. The father and son built a similar log cabin to the one they had lived in previously. Following this move, Abraham constructed a second flatboat and made another trip down the river, but this time as an independent contractor. He then lived on his own, moving in 1831 to New Salem, Illinois.

Lincoln stood out from the crowd as a young man, being six feet four inches tall and lanky. After arriving in New Salem, he obtained employment as a clerk in a general store. Following this, Lincoln began to make a name for himself when he defeated the town bully and surprised most of his neighbours with his strength and ability to split rails and felled trees, a survival skill that he had developed as a child on the American frontier. In small towns of that era, the general store was a place where people met, so Lincoln became intimately familiar with the community. Many people were enchanted by Lincoln's wit, intelligence, and integrity. As one of the few literate citizens of New Salem, Abe's ability to read and write was invaluable. It wasn't long before he became a popular member of the town and was known as a good-natured and 'bookish' young man.

Lincoln's 'failures'

A sample of the so-called Lincoln failures list is shown below. People often use Lincoln's example of overcoming life's struggles or 'failures' to inspire themselves to overcome their own difficulties.

- lost job in 1832
- defeated for state legislature in 1832

- failed in business in 1833
- elected to state legislature in 1834
- sweetheart died in 1835
- had nervous breakdown in 1836
- defeated for speaker in 1838.
- defeated for nomination for Congress in 1843
- elected to Congress in 1846
- lost re-nomination in 1848
- rejected for a land officer in 1849
- defeated for U.S. Senate in 1854
- defeated for nomination for vice president in 1856
- again, defeated for U.S. Senate in 1858
- elected president in 1860

A baby will fall down a lot when she's learning to walk. However, any mother will wholeheartedly affirm to you that her baby will walk one day. Maybe she'll fall down a few times, but she'll walk.

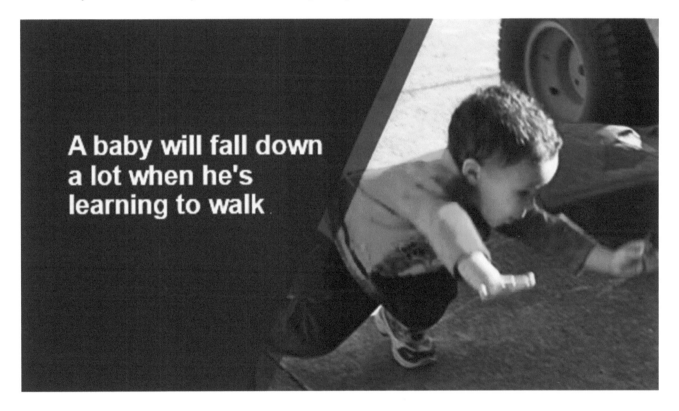

A baby will fall down
a lot when he's
learning to walk.

Most of us don't realise what it took for some people to get where they are in life. They fell many times while learning to walk, just like a baby learning to walk.

Thomas Edison's failures

I didn't fail 1,000 times—the light bulb was an invention with 1,000 steps.

Thomas A. Edison

Thomas Edison famously failed nearly one thousand times to create a commercially viable electric light bulb; but with each failure, he learned about one more avenue that didn't work. After nearly one thousand failed attempts, he eventually succeeded, thanks to the accumulated knowledge he gained from them.

Many of Edison's innovative ideas and inventions are legendary, making him one of the most recognisable names in inventive history. His patents numbered more than one thousand, a record only broken recently, and he invented many ground-breaking technologies, such as the electric light bulb, phonograph, and batteries.

Edison, however, failed often despite his outstanding success. To perfect his experiments, he sometimes had to make thousands of attempts—literally. The same thing happened when Edison was attempting to devise a new storage battery. Walter S. Mallory said Edison had already performed nine thousand experiments but still hadn't found a solution. Upon hearing Mallory's complaint about a lack of results, Edison replied, 'Results! Well, I got lots of results! There are thousands of things that won't work.'

Michael Jordan's failures

In his career, Michael Jordan missed more than nine thousand shots. Almost three hundred of his games ended in defeat. Despite being trusted to take game-winning shots twenty-six times, he failed. Despite failing repeatedly in his life, he eventually became extremely successful in his career.

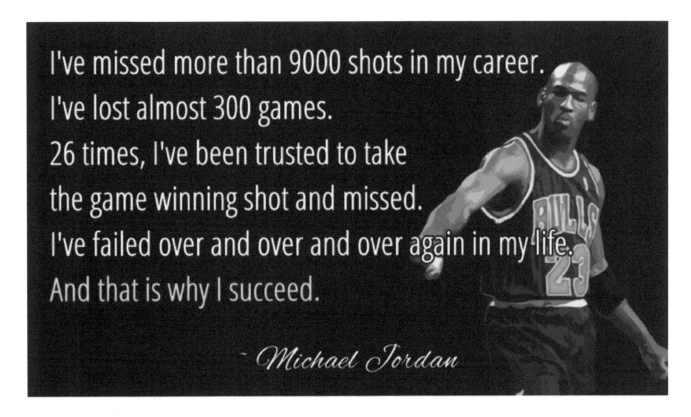

I've missed more than 9000 shots in my career.
I've lost almost 300 games.
26 times, I've been trusted to take
the game winning shot and missed.
I've failed over and over and over again in my life.
And that is why I succeed.

~ *Michael Jordan*

We tend to celebrate the successes and forget the epic journeys towards success that are filled with trials, tribulations, setbacks, and failures. They aren't glamorous to talk about.

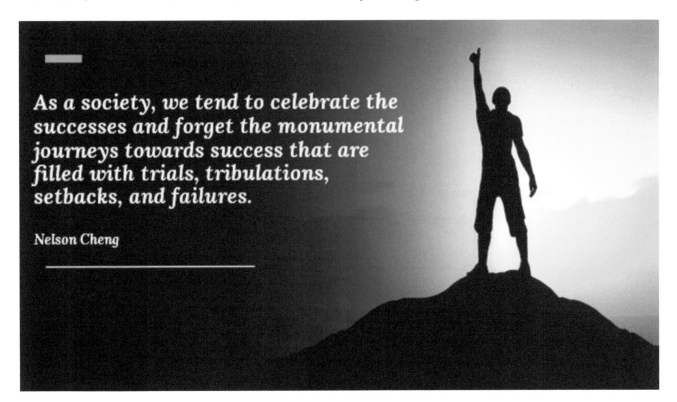

As a society, we tend to celebrate the successes and forget the monumental journeys towards success that are filled with trials, tribulations, setbacks, and failures.

Nelson Cheng

19
CHAPTER

Reflection on Failure as a Lesson in Life

Failure is an invaluable lesson experience

One of the most important lessons learned from failure is experience. If we fail, what happens then? We gain a deeper understanding of life when we experience something for the first time, and then we walk away from it with first-hand experience.

Failing at something is an invaluable experience. It completely alters our mindset through the induction of pain. As we reflect on the real nature of things and their importance to our lives, we transform and improve ourselves.

Failure is a continuum of knowledge accumulation

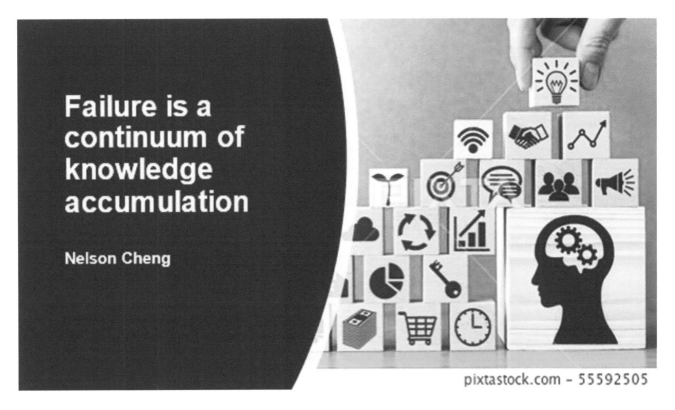

Failure is a continuum of knowledge accumulation

Nelson Cheng

pixtastock.com - 55592505

Failure is an important source of first-hand knowledge. The knowledge gained can be harnessed in the future to overcome the very failure that caused so much pain in the first place. There is nothing more valuable than the knowledge gained from failure.

One of the best examples we get is from Thomas Edison, who famously failed nearly one thousand times to create a commercially viable electric light bulb. With each failure, he gained the knowledge of just one more avenue that didn't work. As a result of numerous failures, he eventually succeeded in inventing the light bulb because of accumulated knowledge.

Failure is a lesson in building resiliency

Resilience is built through failure. Failure makes us more resilient. We must know resilience if we are to achieve great success. We're sure to set ourselves up for a far more painful failure if we think we'll succeed on our first try, or even on the first few tries.

We can benefit so much from the characteristic of resilience during our lives. Having resilience establishes the environment for success. It is no longer assumed that things will happen overnight but that true success will take an enormous amount of effort.

Failure accelerates our maturation

Human beings grow and mature when they fail. In this process, we discover deeper meanings and understandings about our lives and why we do what we do. By reflecting on painful situations, we can develop meaning from them.

We are designed to grow and improve throughout our lives. Growing is a fundamental part of who we are, both as individuals and as a society on a global scale. Without it, we couldn't improve life on every level.

Failure teaches valuable lessons

The most important lesson that can be learned from life's failures is the necessity to create and spread an extraordinary amount of value. It is true that value is at the core of success, and the absence of value is the foundation of failure.

When analysing your past failures, do not forget to consider how much value you brought to the table. Was there a way to enhance the value you brought? If so, would that have prevented failure? If you learn how to consistently create immense value, you will eventually succeed.

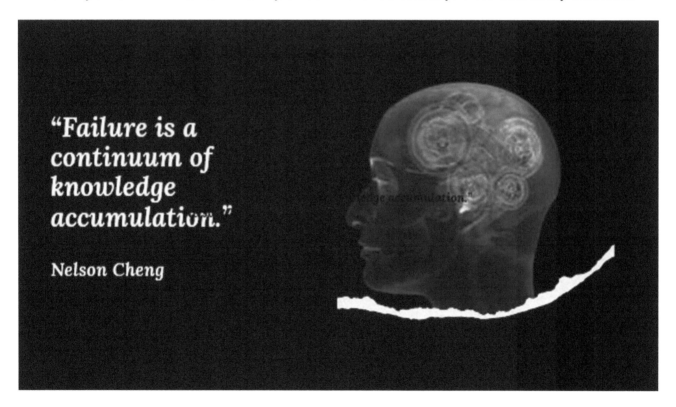

"Failure is a continuum of knowledge accumulation."

Nelson Cheng

20
CHAPTER

Recovering from Failure

You haven't failed yet unless you quit.
—Nelson Cheng

It is possible to recover from failure in a variety of ways. Learning what failure is and how it can help us instead of hindering us will enable us to open our hearts and minds to learn from experiencing the lesson of failure.

The significance of failure is hard to recognise when we're going through it. It's hard to see the forest for the trees. In other words, if you've failed in life, hopefully you now fully understand the importance lesson of failing. The question is, how do you recover from failure? To accomplish this, there is more than one method.

Negative people should be ignored

Surely when you fail, there will be those who will say, 'I told you so' or 'You should have listened to me.' You should ignore them. Don't listen to the critics' otherwise, you will be more discouraged.

People who never make any mistakes are people who never move out of their comfort zones. They will never accomplish much in their lives.

At the end of their life's journey, many will say, 'I should have a try.'

Understand that it's OK to fail sometimes

I think the best way to get over failure is to understand that it's OK to fail. Any search on the Web will bring up dozens of stories about failure from the world's most successful people. There is no shame in failing as long you don't quit.

Failure is a part of life. You won't succeed unless you keep trying. You will taste success when you achieve it. Pushing forward and not giving up is one of the best ways to recover from failure. Remember, it's not a true failure unless you throw in that proverbial towel and wholeheartedly give up forever.

Use failure as a learning opportunity

You can use failure in your life to not only recover from it but also propel you forward. A failure can be one of the greatest platforms for growth in business that is simply unmatched.

It is necessary to illuminate your failures to leverage them. Write out what went wrong and why. Did your past goals have enough relevance? Were there any things you could have done differently?

When you face failures in the future, how will you handle them? What can you learn from the past to help you shape a bigger, brighter future?

If you don't give up, failure isn't the end of the road. In this situation, if you still believe in your goals, you can use failure as a lever to push past your past limitations.

Review your goals

In the past, did you have clear and concrete goals? Was there a smarter way to set goals? Review your past goals and see how clear they were. How precise and exact were they? Could you envision them in your head?

It is possible to fail if you don't set your goals properly. Goals must not only be set correctly but also tracked and analysed regularly on a weekly, daily, and monthly basis.

If you want to recover from failure, re-evaluate your goals. Identify where you need to adjust and spend time analysing.

Create a comprehensive action plan

How do you recover from failure? Make a comprehensive action plan. Lay out a strategy for achieving your goals. Next time you face failure, what will you do?

We have a systematic way of achieving the goals we set for ourselves when we have a comprehensive action plan. We can approach things more long term once we realise that those goals won't be easy to achieve.

Create an action plan that will help you make it past the stumbling blocks of life, and watch as you slowly but surely recover from any setbacks, upsets, or failures.

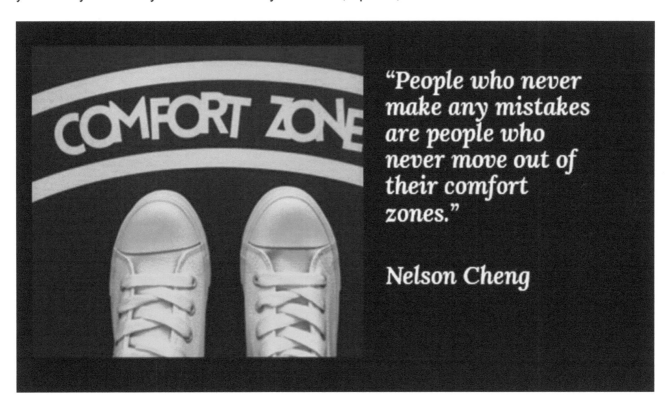

You can't fail if you keep trying.
—Nelson Cheng

21
CHAPTER

Reflection on Simplicity in Life

Definition of simplicity

The state of being simple, uncomplicated, or uncompounded.

What is a life of simplicity?

Living a simpler life means being less hectic and shallow. Understanding simplicity allows you to appreciate things you may have overlooked in the past. The little things in life can create some of the greatest joys in life.

What are the benefits of simplicity?

"It is the simple removal of the unnecessary that makes life simple"
Nelson Cheng

Making decisions is easy. A major advantage of simplifying your life is recognising the right path more easily. Living from a simple yet powerful point of principle will make decisions very clear, no matter how complex the situation is. Making decisions will no longer be a struggle or an issue of confusion.

What is the value of simplicity?

Appreciating the small things in life is the essence of simplicity. Simplicity prevents waste, maintains the economy, and avoids value clashes complicated by greed, fear, peer pressure, and a false sense of identity.

What is the core value of simplicity?

Whatever industry you are associated with, simplicity makes life easier. People tend to favour simplicity and prefer products and experiences that minimise cognitive load. They seek out the least complicated products and services.

What is the core value of life?

The core value of life is simply your core beliefs about life. What you do, what you think, and how you behave are influenced by them. Their values give meaning to your life. This helps you to remember what is important to you and what you would like to achieve in your life.

Why is it beneficial to keep things simple?

Data overload makes life complicated. Thus, keeping it simply means being selective and protective about what you watch, read, listen to, and discuss. As much as possible, you're supposed to filter out the things that are good for you and reduce the negative impact of those that cannot be prevented.

Benefits of simplifying your life by effective time management and gaining control of it

When you manage your time effectively, you become more focused and productive. Being more focused allows you to maximise your potential. As a result, you can spend more time on the projects, goals, and people that matter. Managing your time effectively will help you achieve greater focus and prioritisation.

It can help you reduce stress and prioritise your tasks. Clarifying your goals and prioritising your work is the key to managing your time effectively. As a result, you've got more time to accomplish more.

Manage your time by planning your day, and you'll be more productive. You'll be more efficient. Planning your time is essential to time management. Being productive and effective comes from planning. Establishing your daily priorities will help you make better use of your time. By identifying your priorities, you can spend your most productive time working on them.

Procrastination can be reduced.

People procrastinate when they don't manage their time. You're more likely to procrastinate when you're not clear about your goals. Bad time management makes you procrastinate. Effective time management and managing your time will keep you from procrastinating. Maintaining control over your time helps you to avoid procrastination.

You won't procrastinate if you develop effective time management skills. Being in control of your time helps you stop procrastinating because you feel in control.

You are less likely to procrastinate when you feel focused and in control of your time. You spend more time working on your top priorities when you are clear and focused on your goals.

Distractions are reduced.

As a result of effective time management. When distracted, you are less productive. Focus increases because of effective time management. Managing your time allows you to plan and prioritise better. This allows you to schedule your most important tasks. Most effective time managers set aside chunks of time for their most important tasks. Also, they limit their time more effectively to improve their focus. Clearer boundaries allow you to focus on your top priorities.

They also reduce feeling overwhelmed and having distractions. Feeling overwhelmed occurs when you have too much to do.

There's more time to think.

The benefits of effective time management include more time for planning and thinking. You can work on your top priorities with more time if you plan your time. You can focus on achieving your goals when you have more time to strategise.

Your biggest goals are unlikely to be achieved if you have poor time management skills. As important as acting is taking time to think about how you can achieve your goals.

Effective time management ensures you have time for strategic and creative planning. By doing so, you will be more focused and productive with your time.

List at least two things you are happy about and two things you are frustrated with every day. Imagine how you might do more of what you like while eliminating what frustrates you.

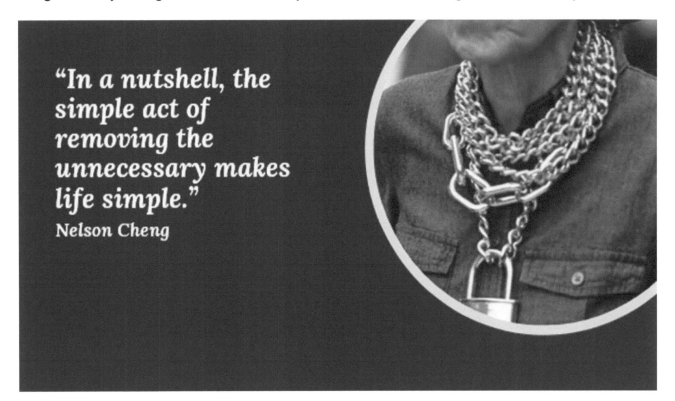

"In a nutshell, the simple act of removing the unnecessary makes life simple."
Nelson Cheng

22
CHAPTER

Reflection on Honesty

The foundation of a successful relationship is trust, and honesty is the basis for it.
—Nelson Cheng

Honesty is the foundation of a good relationship.

Nelson Cheng

A relationship cannot function and thrive without honesty, and trust is the foundation for a successful relationship. By being honest with someone, you show them that you can be trusted. They know that they can rely on your promises and commitments.

Over the last thirty more years of business, I have built good relationships with many of my customers and distributors globally based on the principle of honesty. It is our company's credo that never over-promise and under-deliver; instead, we must deliver what we promised. There were a few occasions that our staff underquoted our customers, but we honoured what we quoted. By adhering to this principle, we have established a reputation as a reliable company in the market, and as such, more than 90 per cent of our business comes from repeat customers.

The importance of honesty

Being honest means refusing to steal, cheat, lie, or deceive in any way. We build character strength when we are honest, which will enable us to serve others and God. Peace of mind and self-respect are blessings, and we will be trusted by the Lord and others.

There is no doubt that honesty is one of the most important qualities in life. It gives you peace of mind where you do not have to worry about the lies that you tell. If you are honest, you will always be respected and trusted by others. In addition, honesty strengthens relationships and creates more meaningful connections between people.

Honour begins with honesty, and honesty is the basis of all high character. Those who are guided by a principle of virtue and honour as their internal basis will act with a dignity and boldness that are impossible for those who are guided only by their own interests.

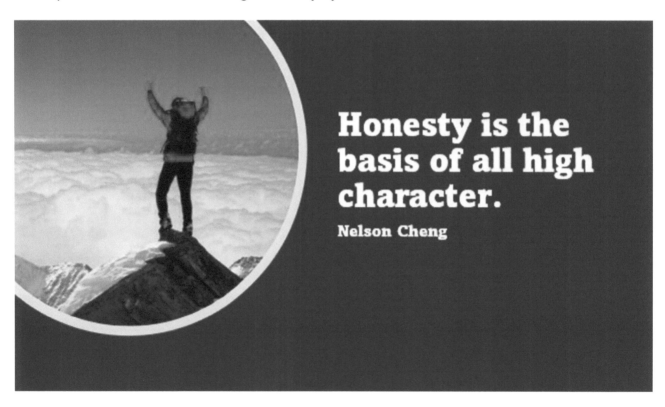

It is costly to be honest, but it pays dividends if you keep sowing it.'
—Nelson Cheng

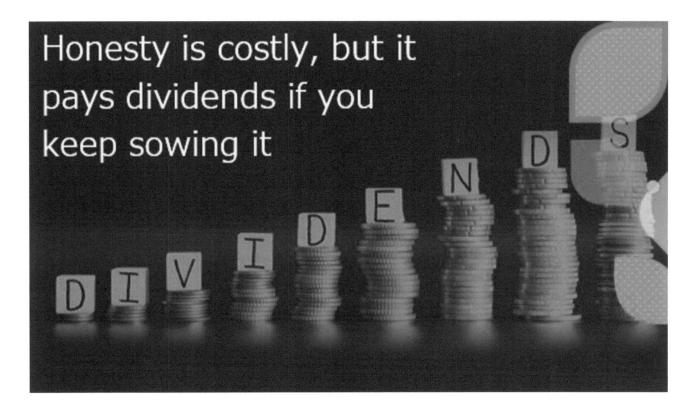

The benefits of honesty

The
virtue of
honesty
fosters
sincerity

Nelson Cheng

The virtue of honesty helps in developing good attributes such as kindness, discipline, truthfulness, moral integrity, etc.

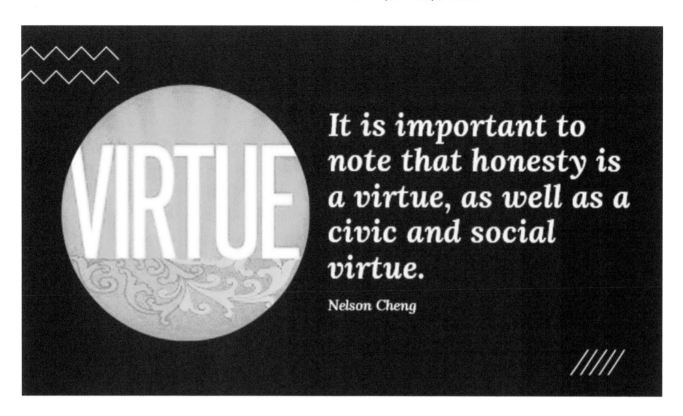

It is important to note that honesty is a virtue, as well as a civic and social virtue.

Nelson Cheng

Honesty is a virtue because it means seeking out the truth, recognising it, holding oneself and others accountable to it, and conforming one's conduct to it.

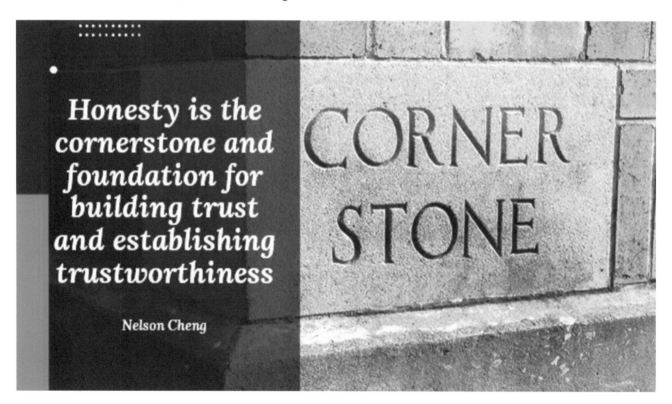

Honesty is the cornerstone and foundation for building trust and establishing trustworthiness

Nelson Cheng

Being honest is a moral duty, which is why we must speak and act in a way that earns and justifies the trust of others.

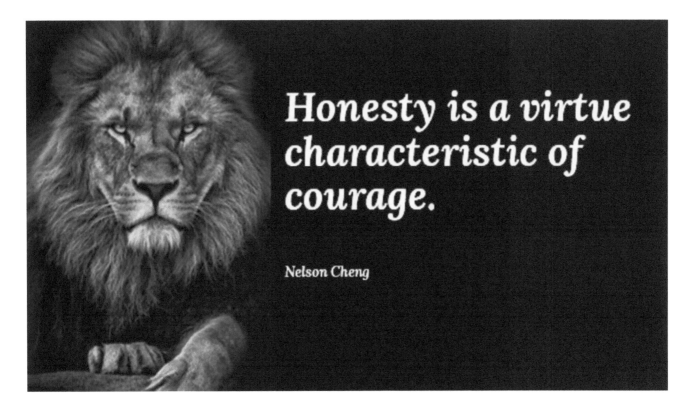

Honesty is one of the strongest character traits you can have.

It is about being true to yourself and others, being genuine and sincere, and speaking the truth. It is evident when someone shares their vulnerabilities.

Honesty is a commendable quality

Honest people are always respected by their peers. Those who have a reputation for being honest have nothing to fear from the world. His candour will be appreciated by all the other people. Those with such character and conduct are respected.

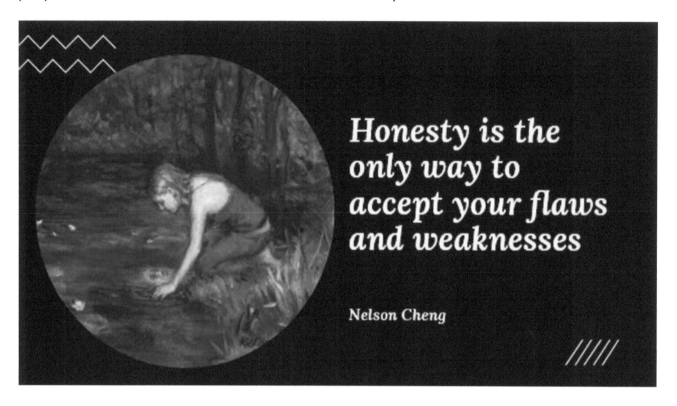

Being true to oneself, to truth, is important not only for individuals but also for society. Truthfulness allows us, as individuals, to grow and mature, learning from our mistakes. Keeping the truth makes social bonds, and keeping the lie and hypocrisy breaks them.

What is the impact of honesty on society?

This implies respecting others, being honest, and being aware of one's own capabilities. In addition to being the basis for trust and the cornerstone of social relationships, honesty gives us hope, confidence, and compassion as well as improves our ability to make decisions.

Should we tell the truth even if it hurts?

To honour truth, one must bear one's own pain without medicating, denying, or blaming it on others. As strange as it may seem, you might find that allowing yourself to experience difficult emotions such as sadness, anger, and disappointment feels better than trying to fend them off, which can lead to suffering in the long run.

What makes the truth so painful?

When we face the truth, we must confront something we have been in denial about. It is possible for you to feel dejected, angry, ashamed, or any number of other emotions. As a result of feeling exposed, the truth can hurt.

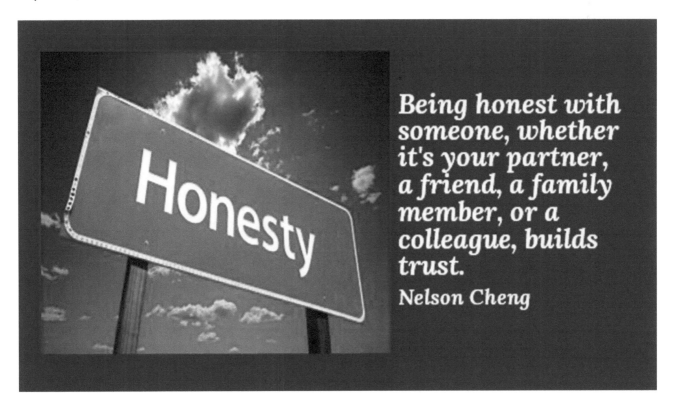

Being honest with someone, whether it's your partner, a friend, a family member, or a colleague, builds trust.
Nelson Cheng

23
CHAPTER

Reflection on Incredulous Scepticism Attitude

We will be discussing in this chapter why having an incredulous sceptical attitude will rob you of the opportunity of achieving success. Despite the facts presented, it is very difficult to convince an incredulous sceptic. As such, it is better to follow your convictions than to try to convince him to join you.

"The skeptic will remain skeptical while the believer will strive to achieve what he believes"

Nelson Cheng

What is a scepticism attitude?

It is having doubt or a disposition to be sceptical in general or regarding a particular subject or subject matter. It is a general attitude of distrusting or doubting despite proven facts and figures. An incredulous sceptical attitude will prevent you from succeeding.

Those who believe will always strive to accomplish their beliefs, while those with a scepticism attitude will remain sceptical, denying themselves success.

"A skeptic will remain in his skepticism while a believer moves on to achieve what he believes."

Nelson Cheng

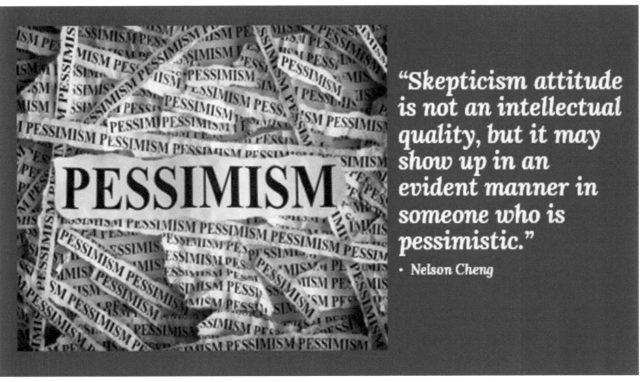

"Skepticism attitude is not an intellectual quality, but it may show up in an evident manner in someone who is pessimistic."

- Nelson Cheng

What makes a person sceptical?

Here are a few signs that a person has a sceptical personality trait: They don't take things at face value. They tend to look for the story behind the story to find out what's really going on. They ask a lot of questions and follow up on any answers that they don't understand or don't seem quite right.

"Doubt and skepticism are good friends, they move in tandem."
Nelson Cheng

24
CHAPTER

Reflection on Ideas

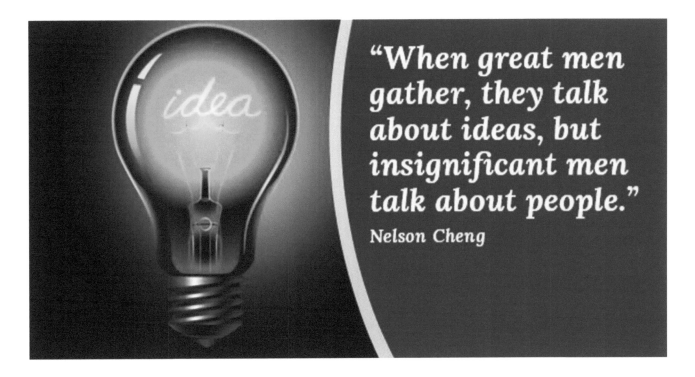

"When great men gather, they talk about ideas, but insignificant men talk about people."
Nelson Cheng

The importance of talking about ideas

For a society to progress, people need to spend more time discussing ideas instead of talking about one another. Society progresses, changes, and develops through ideas. Invention, innovation, and creativity are sparked by ideas for the betterment of society and humanity.

Ideas have a great deal of value

You can make an idea worth its weight in gold by capturing, growing, and developing it. There is no value in a great idea if it is not executed. However, a decent one with good execution is most likely to generate some profit. There are doors in ideas because they can lead to new understandings.

What to do with the idea you conceived

Keep doing what you're doing, and don't worry about it. It's impossible to please everyone. Before they move beyond their original ideas, many successful ideas seem unworkable or unpopular. What used to sound ridiculous can end up changing the world once they get a life of their own.

What is the process of conceptualising an idea?

Put your mind to work, whatever the focus, and don't be afraid of your thoughts. There is a possibility that you will stumble upon something brilliant. Educating yourself is an opportunity to explore and let your mind wander. What will your ideas contribute to the past, what will they contribute to the future, or nothing at all?

The essentials of generating valuable ideas

Our ability to generate valuable ideas depends on observing certain essentials.

Connectivity

It is becoming increasingly important for things to be connected.

If you can connect more things, then your ideas are likely to be better and will be more refined. Consequently, your ability to come up with good ideas depends heavily on the quality and quantity of connections that you can make.

Taking a macro idea generation

To improve idea generation, think about things from a macro perspective. You can zoom your perspective out to a macro level no matter what you learn if you see how it relates to other things you are trying to brainstorm.

Idea capture should be done as soon as possible

There is no set time when ideas will come to you; they just appear when they choose to do so.

You can't just prepare for your next brainstorming session by training yourself to come up with better ideas. It is, instead, important to recognise that ideas constantly come to you and to develop the habit of acknowledging and capturing them.

Discover a simple way to capture your ideas now when they come to you.

Don't let that idea slip by without recording it in a notebook or on the note section of your mobile phone or leaving yourself a voicemail or sending yourself an email.

Problem-solving ideas should be the focus

Solving problems for people is what makes an idea valuable.

Think about what problems people have that you'd like to solve rather than waiting for a magical idea to strike.

This inversion process focuses your idea generation and increases your chances of coming up with a good idea.

Your ideas will instantly be more valuable if you do this.

"When you speak an idea, something happens that doesn't happen when you write it."
Nelson Cheng

25

CHAPTER

Reflection on Delayed Gratification and Its Importance

We live in an age where one-click purchases and instant access to information are the norms. As a result of smartphones and Wi-Fi, we live in an always-on world where we must get what we want right away. Although instant gratification can be tempting, impulse control is an essential life skill. Delayed gratification is the key to achieving your goals.

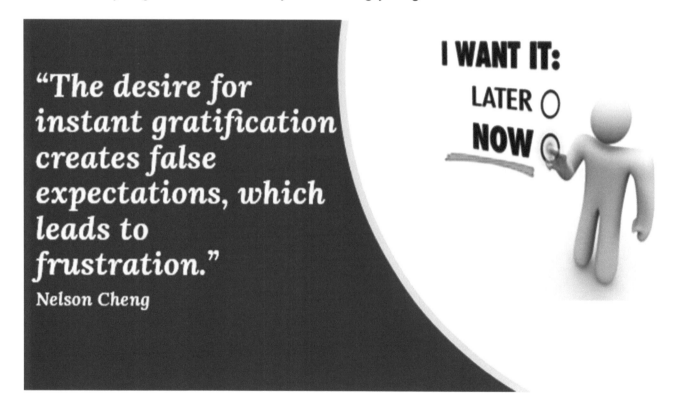

"The desire for instant gratification creates false expectations, which leads to frustration."
Nelson Cheng

Getting everything, you want isn't realistic, and getting it immediately isn't even possible. The desire for instant gratification creates false expectations, which leads to frustration. Using delayed gratification allows you to strategise thoughtfully and learn from your mistakes. How does delayed gratification work? What are the best ways to develop this essential skill? These will be discussed in this chapter.

What is delayed gratification?

It is defined as having the ability to postpone an immediate gain for a greater and more rewarding reward later. In many Asian cultures, delaying gratification is seen as a central part of this ability to resist temptation and stick to our goals. By delaying what we want now, we may end up with something better later.

Delaying gratification is also related to other self-regulation skills, such as patience, impulse control, self-control, and willpower. An individual's capacity to regulate his or her own behaviour is referred to as self-regulation.

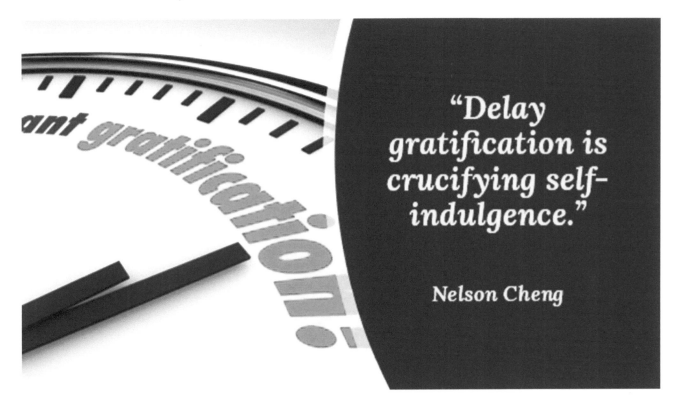

"Delay gratification is crucifying self-indulgence."

Nelson Cheng

How can delayed gratification be demonstrated?

A major challenge in many aspects of life is choosing long-term rewards over immediate gratification. Our ability to delay gratification can mean the difference between achieving our goals and not achieving them, whether we are trying to lose weight or studying instead of going out to a party.

Here are examples of delayed gratification: saving money for retirement rather than spending it now; not finishing all the food on the plate because you want to save room for dessert; a parent giving their child a cookie after they have done their chores.

How instant gratification keeps you from achieving your goals

It is common to hear advice like 'Live in the moment' or 'The time is now.' These are wise words and being aware of the present moment is a good way to live. We may not necessarily benefit from getting everything we want at the time we want it.

Fast information, fast food, fast technology, fast entertainment, fast comfort—we have it all. In many cases, we can purchase goods and services in an instant that will satisfy our every need without having to exert too much effort.

The lessons and benefits we miss out on when we don't delay fulfilment are what we don't consider. The harder work we put into achieving satisfaction, the more personal growth we experience. It is also commonplace for us to take for granted the importance of aiming for long-term goals and gaining satisfaction through the process.

As a result of instant gratification, you just want to purchase things instantly even though you may not have the budget for them; hence, you buy on credit, which results in debt, clutter, bad health, distractions, and mindlessness; whereas restraint and conscious lead to simplicity, health and fitness, focus, achievement, mindfulness, and appreciation for life's gifts.

It is easy to become detached from our core values and important things in life in a world of luxury and technology. The importance of superficial things increases objects, material wealth, acquisition, and appearance. It is no longer necessary for us to acknowledge the future and the possible consequences of our actions, and all these can keep us from achieving our long-term goals because of instant gratification.

How to practice delayed gratification

Restraint and mindfulness are the keys to making good decisions—being aware of our decisions and having boundaries.

An essential life skill is the ability to wait for a better reward later. It is possible to delay gratification in many ways, such as putting off large purchases for a vacation, skipping dessert to lose weight, or taking on a job you do not necessarily enjoy but will benefit your career in the future.

Don't lose sight of your goals. If delayed gratification is not about achieving your biggest dreams and goals, then what is? To achieve the body of your dreams and to have more energy, you put off that purchase to save for a home or retirement. To remind yourself of what you're working towards, keep a picture of your goal on your phone—even as your wallpaper. This will make delayed gratification a lot easier.

The benefits of delayed gratification

Rather than purchasing something you do not need right now, delay your gratification until later, and you will reap the benefits of having more savings and financial freedom in the long run. The delayed gratification of compounding your money is even greater when you make investments.

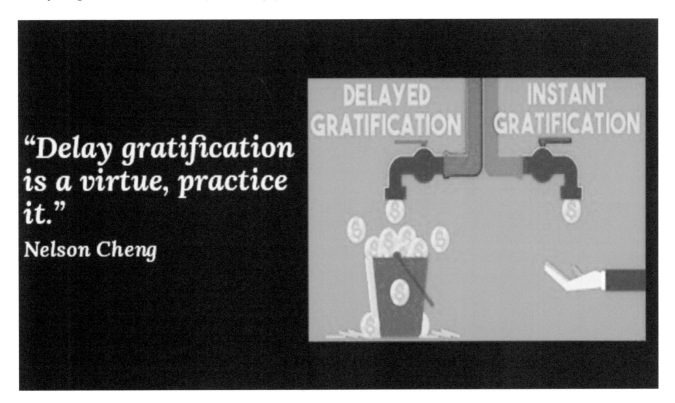

"Instant gratification can lead to excessive spending, while delayed gratification can help in wealth accumulation."

Nelson Cheng

26
CHAPTER

Reflection on Passion

It is passion that keeps us going, that fills us with meaning, happiness, excitement, and anticipation. Having a passion for work and life is a powerful force that will help you succeed in whatever you set your mind to.

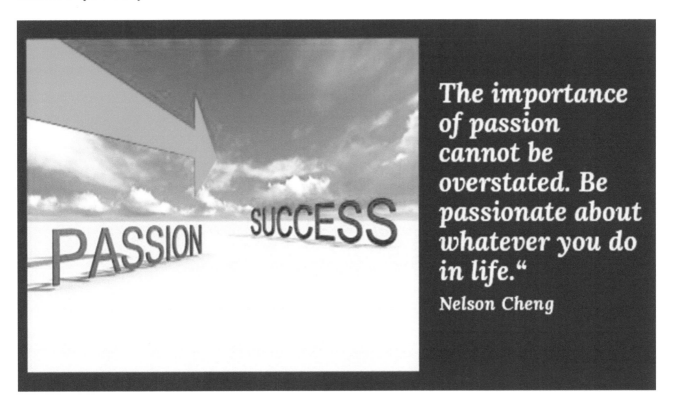

The importance of passion cannot be overstated. Be passionate about whatever you do in life."
Nelson Cheng

We can all live better lives when we are driven by passion. Dreams can only be achieved with passion. You will effortlessly reach rarefied heights when you identify your passion and align it with whatever you're doing. It becomes enjoyable and joyful to work. We often go unnoticed by the passing of the hours. In pursuit of greater achievements, fatigue and tiredness take a back seat.

What is passion, and what is purpose?

Passion is a combination of emotions, motivation, and what makes us feel good—that is, 'Do what you love.' Purpose is what motivates us to do what we do, primarily for the benefit of others—that is, 'Do what contributes.' Passion may be all over the place, wild and exciting, but purpose is much more focused.

What makes passion so important in life?

A passion gives you a reason to keep learning and to work towards mastery. It can often give you a reason to travel and, therefore, to have the new experiences that are key to happiness. It gives you something in common with other people and so fosters social bond.

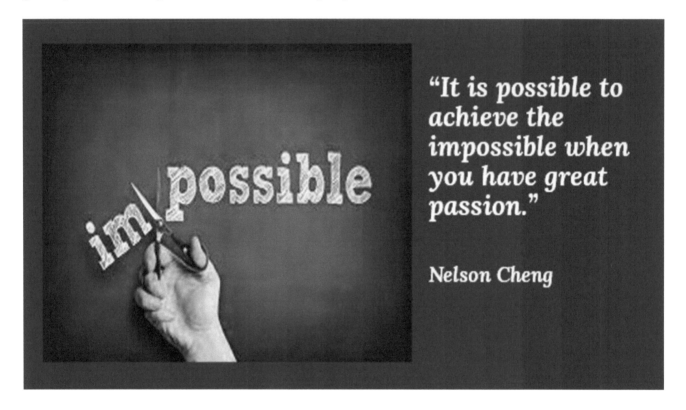

"It is possible to achieve the impossible when you have great passion."

Nelson Cheng

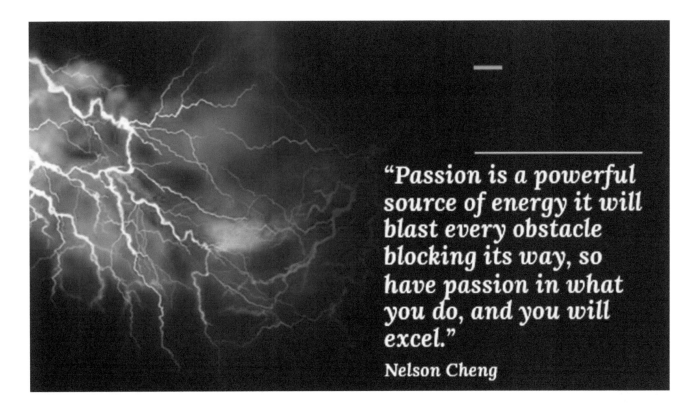

"Passion is a powerful source of energy it will blast every obstacle blocking its way, so have passion in what you do, and you will excel."

Nelson Cheng

How does passion affect your life?

You learn more and work towards mastery when you are passionate about what you do. As a result, it gives you a sense of direction.

When faced with obstacles, people who are enthusiastic and passionate tend to be more resilient. When people are passionate about what they do, they are more likely to have a positive outlook and overcome problems rather than doing only what they do for money.

27
CHAPTER

Reflection on Meaning of Life

Is there more to life?

Invest in your future by studying hard, finding a good job, climbing the corporate ladder, buying a house, and teaching your children the same values. Often, we follow these things haphazardly, wondering, 'Is there more to life?'

"The challenge of human existence is not just staying alive but finding meaning in life."
Nelson Cheng

One of the most meaningful things in life is to bring light to the darkest moments of someone's life by giving hope to their situations.

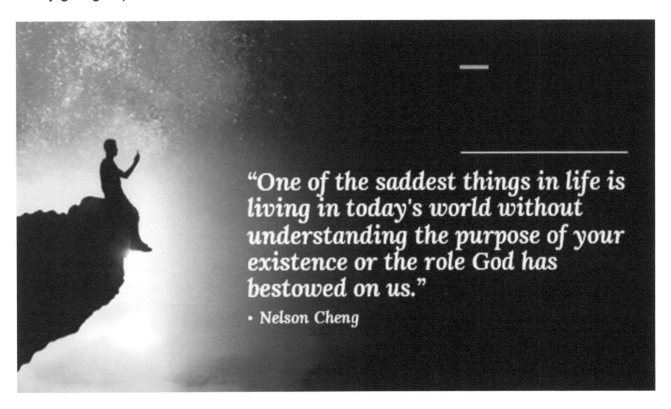

When we work ourselves to the bone for money and fame, and gain lots of material things without understanding the truth of our existence, our lives are so empty and painful; and even when we do have money, name, and gain, isn't everything just as empty if we do not know the purpose of our existence?

"Don't waste your time living or imitating someone else's life, our time on earth is limited. Know the purpose of your existence and fulfil it."

Nelson Cheng

Living a meaningful is simply to touch the lives of as many people as possible and to know the role that God has bestowed upon you by fulfilling it.

28

CHAPTER

Reflection on Hope

Why hope is important in life

Having hope means hoping for some positive outcome to improve your life. By envisioning a better future, we are motivated to take the steps to achieve it, not only to make a bad situation better but also to make our lives better in the long run.

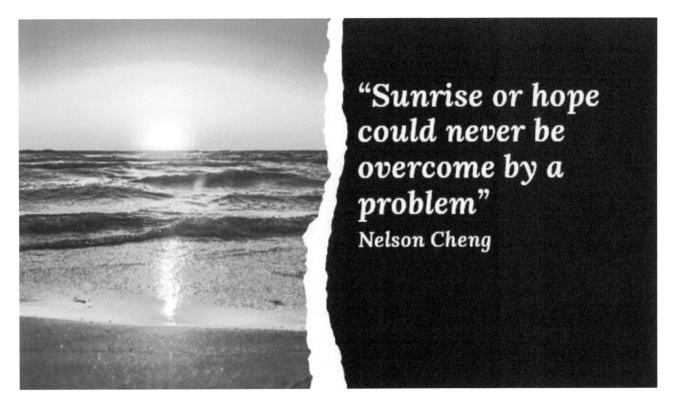

"Sunrise or hope could never be overcome by a problem"
Nelson Cheng

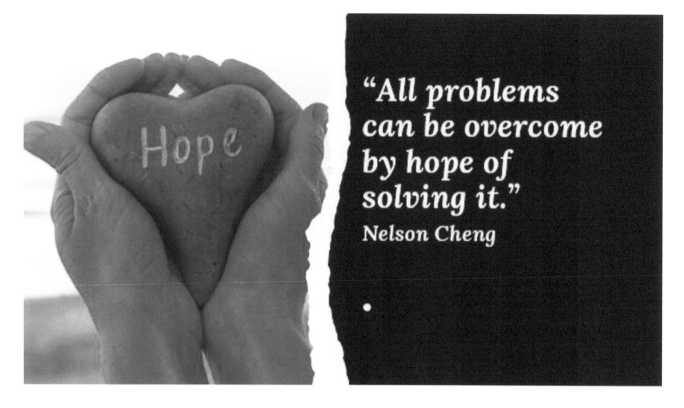

As the saying goes, 'Hope is the ability to see the light despite the darkness.' There was no problem that could defeat sunrise or hope.

Everyone lives with hope whether they realise it. Hope is something we all hold on to. As human beings, it is part of who we are. In our minds, hope plays an important role in defining what we want in our futures and contributing to our self-narrative about our lives.

"Despite the harshest environments, hope to survive will enable you to thrive."
Nelson Cheng

Hoping to survive will provide a way for you to thrive even in the most hostile environment.

"There is always hope for the future, even for people who are pessimistic."

Nelson Cheng

Even the most pessimistic person can have hope for the future.

What is the importance of hope?

Hope is wanting a result that will improve your life in some way. By envisioning a better future, it can not only make a tough present situation more bearable but also motivate you to take steps to bring it about.

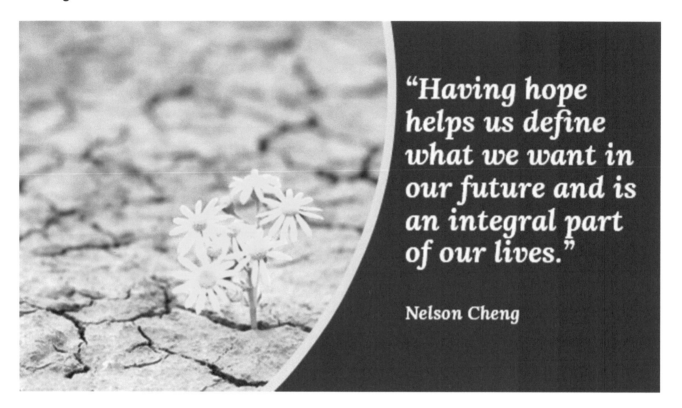

"Having hope helps us define what we want in our future and is an integral part of our lives."

Nelson Cheng

Hope and its importance

It is common for people to associate hope with dire situations. It is human nature to hope for a way out of difficult circumstances. When people do that, they tend to hope fervently! The key to making everyday life better can also be found in hope.

"Hope involves planning and motivation and determination to get what one hopes for."
Nelson Cheng

"To turn your hope into a reality requires planning, motivation, and determination to get one hope for."
Nelson Cheng

29

CHAPTER

Reflection on Challenges of Life

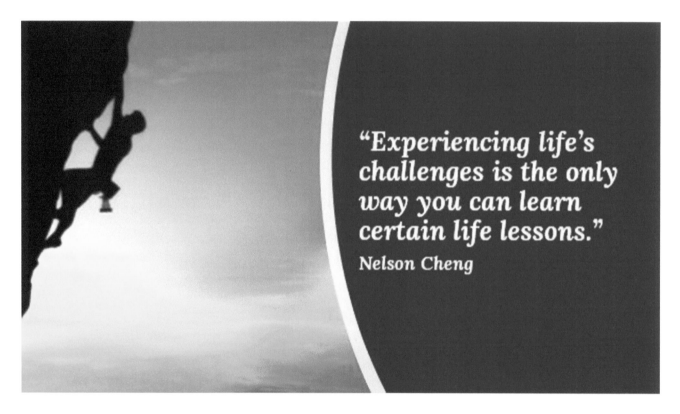

"Experiencing life's challenges is the only way you can learn certain life lessons."
Nelson Cheng

It is inevitable that life will present us with challenges and difficulties that may seem insurmountable or overwhelming. By overcoming them, we can learn a great deal from them.

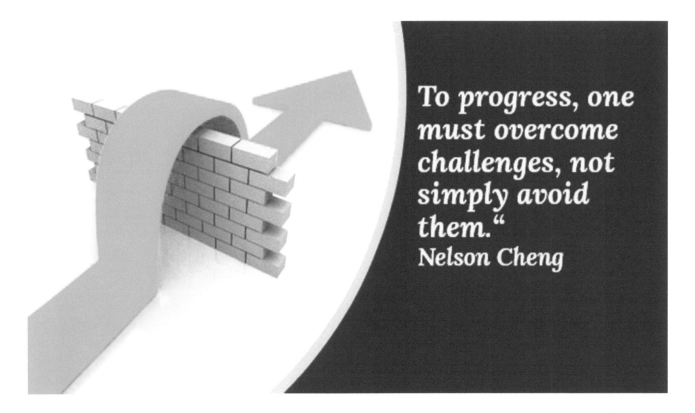

To progress, one must overcome challenges, not simply avoid them."
Nelson Cheng

Life is full of challenges no matter how perfect you think you and your life are. Unless you face and solve challenges, they won't go away. I think it's better to acknowledge your challenge, solve them, and move on with your life than to make it all a big deal. It's important not to allow your challenges to bring you sorrow, hurt, and grief.

Challenges in life should make us stronger, not bitter. To succeed, we must overcome challenges. The challenges you face can make or break you. I hope this chapter on challenges inspires you to become the best you can possibly be. You must never give up.

It is possible for us to run into many barriers and issues while trying to get on with our lives. When we are aware of what we are dealing with, we can do better when we aren't at our full potential. Knowing what problems you have in your life will help you deal with them more effectively.

What are some challenges of life?

Listed below are challenges in life that are most encountered.

These are some of the most common problems each of us will encounter no matter where we go or what we do. These are some of the issues we need to address.

Health challenges

It is inevitable that you will be unwell at some point in your life. Depending on how big and intense it is, it might be something minor or something minor but intense. It could be anything. As our bodies work around the clock, it is common to have health issues because they do fail occasionally. Health crises become worse if not dealt with at the right time, resulting in a variety of other problems. Get to the bottom of any health issue you have instead of pretending it doesn't exist.

Workplace challenges

Everybody works when the opportunity and time arise. Nevertheless, this is the time when you realise whether you can manage teamwork and professional relationships. A workplace is a place where you are expected to perform your duties as outlined in your employment contract. It is possible, however, to face certain challenges that you are not prepared for. At the beginning, these issues may make you feel apprehensive and frustrated, but the best course of action is to address them immediately and resolve them. Instead of leaving the workplace, this is the best course of action.

Career challenges

It is inevitable that you will encounter work-related issues on your journey to success. Along with these issues, you might find it difficult to progress in your career. You can face thousands of problems such as not getting the promotion you hoped for, not getting the job you applied for, and so on. Identify the issues you may have within yourself, such as personal issues or attitude problems, to deal with these issues. Recover and try again after you work on yourself.

Discrimination challenges

There are many people in this world who are unjust and unfair when they are in power. Unless you've encountered anything like that, you're bound to meet such people when you step outside. You shouldn't let this unfair treatment cause you problems or breakdowns. So don't take this too seriously and deal with it as it comes. You will succeed if you are good at what you do.

Challenges of an emotional nature

The term does not refer to serious disorders and diseases. It's these minor issues that we usually ignore and don't deal with because we don't think they're important. As we strive to improve our lives, we forget that mental stress and anxiety are serious issues that require immediate attention.

Peace of mind challenges

Despite being successful in life and doing what you love, there is something that doesn't feel right. You might not yet have the inner peace you seek, and it stresses you out. We all experience it occasionally, and it's not a big deal. All you need to do is find a way to feel different and achieve inner peace through prayers and seeking God's will for your life.

Challenges associated with finances

We live in an uncertain world, and financial crises can strike at any stage of our lives. Financial crises can take you by surprise no matter how prepared you are. When you are hit by a crisis, you may feel frustrated and stressed out. There are many reasons why you might have lost your job, lost your investment, or had a downfall in the business world. It is best to accept the fact that this has happened. Accepting it will allow you to deal with it. Start by identifying what went wrong and what you can do to correct it.

Challenges of failure

It is inevitable that you will face failure while moving forward, achieving your goals, and moving on with your career, but that does not mean that you cannot move forward. It is important to learn from your failures and use them to make yourself a better person in the future. When you learn to deal with failure, you will be able to deal with every obstacle you encounter.

Friendship challenges

It is important to have friends in our lives so that we can spend time together, share sorrows and joys, and just get along with each other. The best part of life is having friends, but sometimes these relationships can be troublesome. There are backstabbing, jealousy, betrayal, and many other things that ruin a friendship, affecting the whole life. This problem is best solved by never opening to friends at first. Move forward with friendships after knowing whom you're dealing with. Keep your interactions with toxic or unhealthy friends to a minimum.

Challenges of feeling empty

Occasionally, your life feels boring, unproductive, and there is nothing you can do about it. This leads to emptiness, which might not seem like a big deal, but it has a huge impact on your life. Even though career-oriented people don't care about their wellness and adventurous aspects of life deeply, it is affecting them and their careers as well. Break out of your routine and do something unusual to overcome boredom and emptiness.

Why it is important to overcome life's challenges

The obstacles we encounter on life's journey must be overcome. Being able to overcome obstacles is important because it allows us to move forward in life without being stifled by our challenges.

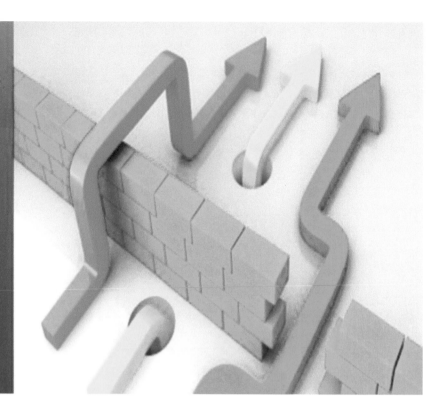

"Being able to overcome obstacles is important because it allows us to move forward in life without being stifled by our challenges."

Nelson Cheng

"Resilient people don't give up easily despite difficulties and are able to overcome them head-on. Even though overcoming obstacles will take time and effort, they stay inspired and motivated, and ultimately achieved their goals."

Nelson Cheng

Growing through life's challenges

Only through constant effort and struggle can strength and growth be achieved.
—Nelson Cheng

When we bow to challenges in life, they become obstacles and hinder our growth as a person.

Worries about the challenges of life often give small challenges a big shadow.

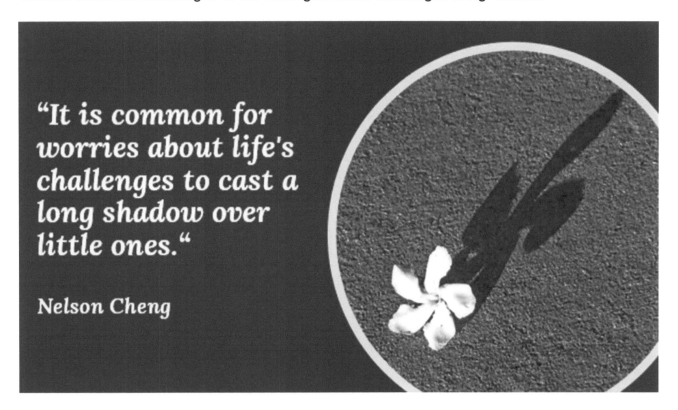

> "It is common for worries about life's challenges to cast a long shadow over little ones."
>
> Nelson Cheng

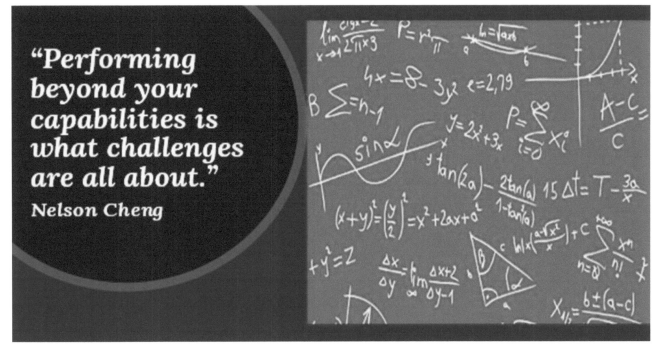

> "Performing beyond your capabilities is what challenges are all about."
>
> Nelson Cheng

Taking on challenges is doing something you aren't qualified to do because fear cannot overcome courage.

We are daring to win tomorrow's rewards by facing today's challenges with courage.

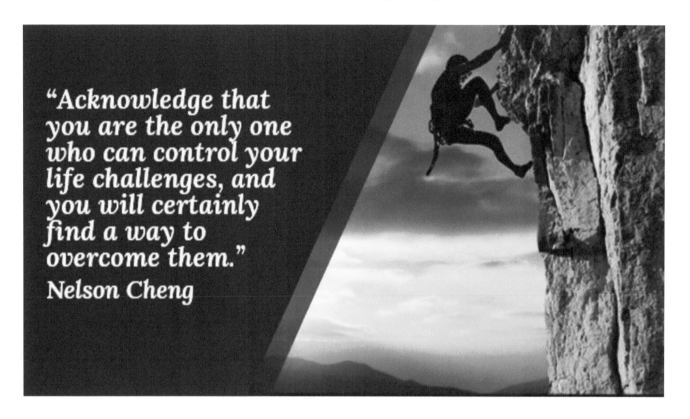

"Acknowledge that you are the only one who can control your life challenges, and you will certainly find a way to overcome them."
Nelson Cheng

To progress, one must overcome challenges, not simply avoid them."
Nelson Cheng

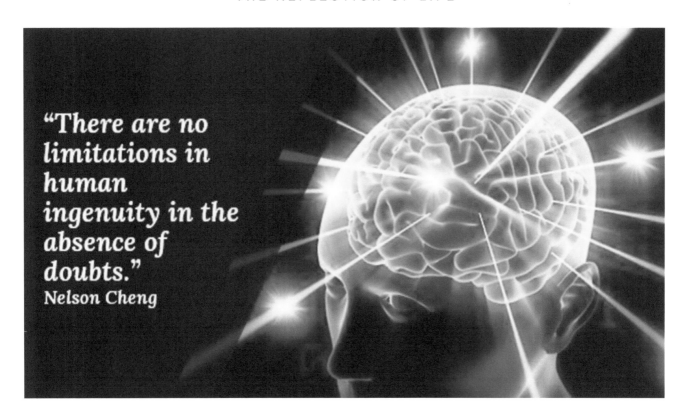

"There are no limitations in human ingenuity in the absence of doubts."
Nelson Cheng

30
CHAPTER

Reflection on Hope

Without hope, people lose motivation to endure their struggles when they cannot visualise the desired outcome.

A powerful emotion that humans experience is hope. Having hope brings us forward in life, provides hope for the future, and makes us feel better about ourselves. In the absence of hope, we may as well give up on life since we will never be able to regain what we have lost.

Despite everything we go through in life, hope gives meaning to life, allows us to understand things we may not have previously understood, and, most importantly, gives us the strength to continue living. Almost everyone would agree that hope cannot exist without trust.

Hope is one of the most powerful forces in the world. During tough times, it inspires us to do the impossible and remain optimistic. Hope can manifest in many ways. It can be helpful to listen to our favourite thought leaders or music.

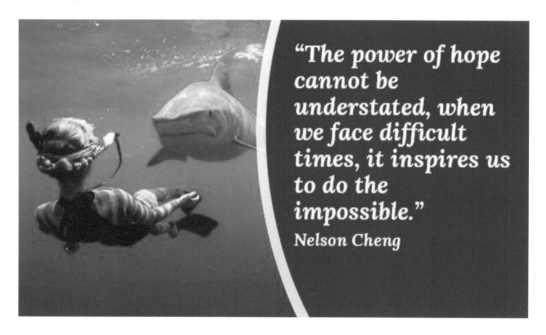

"The power of hope cannot be understated, when we face difficult times, it inspires us to do the impossible."
Nelson Cheng

What is hope?

It can simply be defined as expecting and desiring a particular outcome. There are a variety of definitions of hope, including an expectation or desire that something desired will occur in the future, an object of hope with a particular implication of a positive outcome. The survival of life on earth would be an example of such hope.

When we're sceptical that a positive outcome will occur, hope motivates us to persevere towards our goal or end state. The way to bring about that hope is to strengthen our willpower, boost our persistence, find pathways to our goals and dreams, and look for heroes of hope. We may one day be able to emulate such a hero.

Hope is not something that makes you feel a certain way about life all the time but rather a frame of mind that keeps us going despite all odds. You cannot feel hope without having hope, so it is the strongest emotion.

"When we have hope, we can overcome obstacles and fears because we believe that things will turn out well in the end."
Nelson Cheng

The world would be a much different place if humanity had more hope, even though everyone has their own definition of hope.

How to bolster hope

Get involved in a religious or spiritual community. Knowing that something or someone much larger than oneself exists has helped people find strength, find peace, and elevate their spirits.

"Hope is one of the essential traits of successful people."

Nelson Cheng

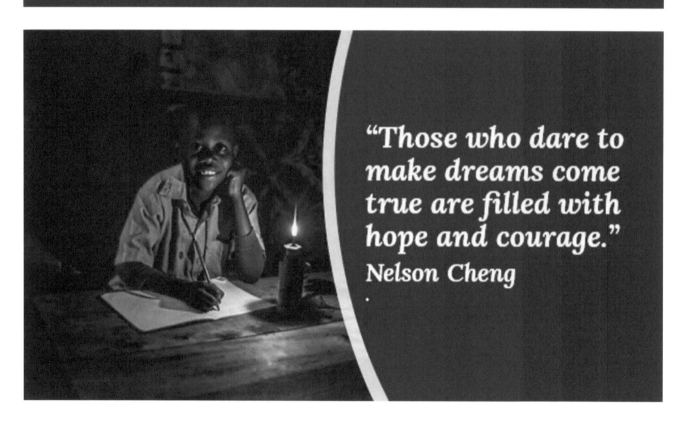

"Those who dare to make dreams come true are filled with hope and courage."
Nelson Cheng

31
CHAPTER

Reflection on Awakening the Sleeping Giant in You

What does it mean to awaken a sleeping giant?

A sleeping giant means that someone or something has great power but has not yet demonstrated it fully. My belief is that everyone has a sleeping giant waiting to be awakened.

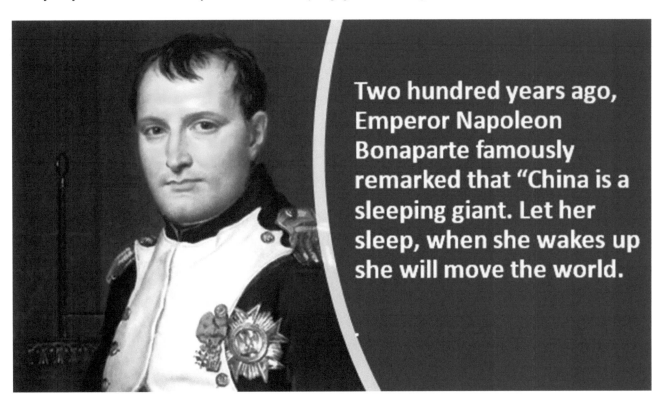

Two hundred years ago, Emperor Napoleon Bonaparte famously remarked that "China is a sleeping giant. Let her sleep, when she wakes up she will move the world.

What happened to China after she has awakened?

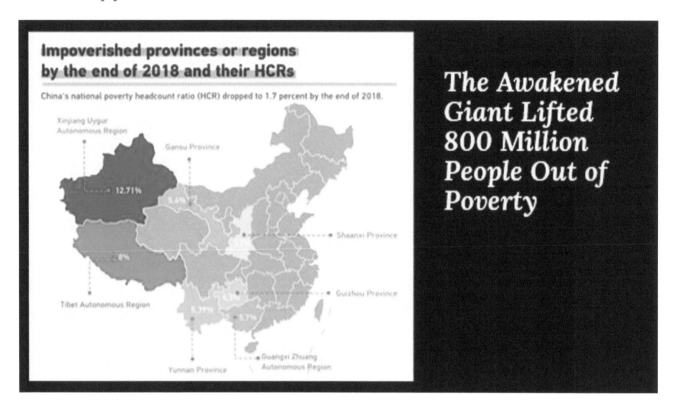

The awakened giant lifted eight hundred million people out of poverty.

Almost eight hundred million people have been lifted out of poverty since 1978 when China began to open and reform its economy. Over the same period, access to health, education, and other services has improved significantly.

Trade, investment, and ideas from China are having an increasing influence on other developing economies. There are many development challenges that China faces that are relevant to other countries, including transitioning to a new growth model, rapid ageing, building cost-effective health systems, and promoting a lower carbon energy pathway.

The awakened giant is the second-largest economy in the world.

The awakened giant is now the second-largest economy in the world, surpassing Japan

China is now the second-largest economy in the world, surpassing Japan. In 2010, Japan's gross domestic product increased by just under 4 per cent, a much slower rate than China's and not enough to keep the economy ahead.

The awakened giant's GDP ranks number one in the world based on purchasing power parity (PPP).

According to the World Bank, China's gross domestic product ranked number one in the world in 2017 based on purchasing power parity.

A purchasing power parity (PPP) compares the absolute purchasing power of currencies and, to some extent, the living standards of people in different countries based on the prices of specific goods. In simple terms, PPP is used for converting one country's currency into another country's currency to purchase the same amount of goods and services.

The awakened giant has the largest navy in the world.

China has the largest navy in the world, and there are more ships in China's navy than anywhere else in the world.

As of early 2020, China has the largest navy in the world with about 350 surface ships and submarines, including more than 130 major surface combatants, according to the '2020 China Military Power Report' published by the Pentagon in September 2020.

The awakened giant built the longest and most extensive high-speed rail.

With a total length of 40,000 kilometres (25,000 mi) by the end of 2021, the People's Republic of China's high-speed rail network will be the longest and most extensively used in the world.

The awakened giant built bullet trains that reaches speeds of up to 350 kmph.

High-speed trains in China, also called bullet trains or fast trains, can reach speeds of 350 kmph (217 mph). A total of 2,800 pairs of bullet trains numbering G, D, or C run daily in China, connecting more than 550 cities across thirty-three of its thirty-four provinces. It takes only 4.5 hours to travel 1,318 km (819 mi) between Beijing and Shanghai by high-speed train.

The awakened giant started the Belt and Road Initiative.

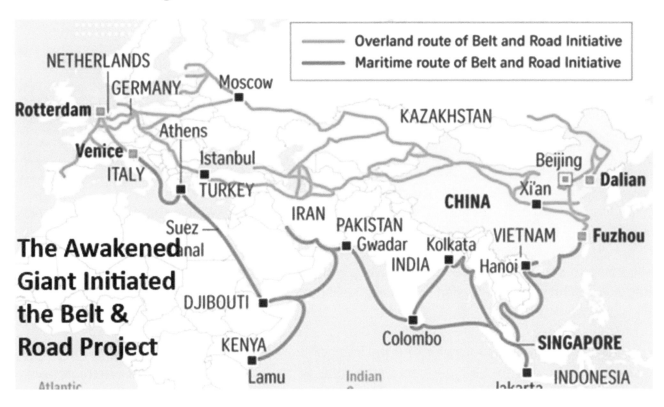

A major infrastructure project, the Belt and Road Initiative (BRI), has been called the New Silk Road by some, which stretches from East Asia to Europe. This vast collection of development and investment initiatives was launched by Chinese president Xi Jinping in 2013. It will significantly expand China's economic and political influence.

The BRI is intended to create an expanded, interdependent market for Chinese goods, to increase China's economic and political influence, and to create the necessary conditions for China to establish a high-tech economy by developing a wide range of products.

The awakened giant becomes the world's leading shipbuilding nation.

The Awakened Giant Becomes the World's Leading Shipbuilding Nation

In the first half of 2022, China led the global shipbuilding industry with a share of 46.2 per cent, multiple indicators showed on Thursday.

According to statistics released by the Ministry of Industry and Information Technology (MIIT), the nation's shipyards completed 18.5 million deadweight tons of orders, taking 45.2 percent of the global market.

By June 30, orders accounted for 47.8 per cent of the market, the largest in the world. Ships for export accounted for 88.7 per cent of the total, with 102.74 million DWT of orders, totalling 102.74 million DWT.

China has maintained its position as the world's leading shipbuilding nation in 2021, according to the statistics released by China Association of the National Shipbuilding Industry (CANSI). China surpasses South Korea as world's number-one shipbuilder in 2021, overtaking South Korea in 2021 to become champion of annual order volume.

According to Clarkson, a British shipbuilding and shipping analyst, the global order volume for new ships in 2021 was 45.73 million compensated gross tons (CGTs), with South Korea receiving 17.35 million CGTs, accounting for 38 per cent, second only to China with 22.8 million.

Statistics from the China Association of the National Shipbuilding Industry show China's in-hand ship orders reached 96.39 million deadweight tons (DWTs) by the end of November 2021, an increase of 35.9 per cent over last year.

The awakened giant leads the way with private 5G networks at industrial facilities.

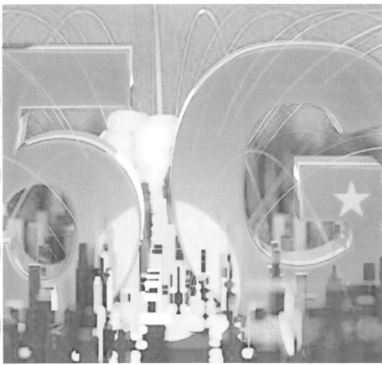

China is widely regarded as the leader in deploying localised high-speed 5G networks in sprawling industrial sites, which aim to automate labour-intensive, dangerous processes and increase productivity.

Mines with 5G Technology.

Mines with 5G technology, factories with internet-connected cameras that process and count freight containers, and seaports with internet-connected cameras that drill and drill remotely are all examples of these sites.

Unlike consumer-oriented 5G networks that cover towns and cities, these private networks are tailored to specific enterprise sites with custom hardware and software. Because of their isolation from public networks, they can be tailored to specific requirements and handle more complex tasks and processes.

The awakened giant files 40.3 per cent of global 6G patent.

China accounted for 40.3 per cent of global 6G patent filings, followed by the U.S. with 35.2 per cent. Japan accounted for 9.9 per cent, Europe accounted for 8.9 per cent, and South Korea accounted for 4.2 per cent.

The awakened giant achieved 6G transmission speed.

According to a statement on its website, Purple Mountain Laboratories' chief scientist Professor You Xiaohu led a team of researchers to achieve sixth-generation (6G) level of wireless transmission through 206.25 gigabits per second for the first time in a lab setting. China Mobile and Fudan University collaborated on the project, which was supported by a special government project on 6G.

Using vortex millimetre waves, a form of extremely high-frequency radio wave with rapidly changing spins, Chinese researchers were able to transmit 1 terabyte of data over 1 km (3,300 feet) in a second.

As a result of their experiment, the team concluded China was 'leading the world' in the research of potential 6G technologies.

The awakened giant launches record number of satellites with Long March 8 rocket.

The Awakened Giant Launches Record Number of Satellites with Long March 8 Rocket

China's two recent rocket launches set a record for the largest number of satellites ever deployed by a Chinese rocket with the launch of a Long March 8 rocket. This expanded the nation's remote sensing capabilities as well as its information and communication technology (ICT) infrastructure.

The awakened giant built 830,000 bridges.

The number of bridges built in China by the end of 2017 exceeded 830,000. China is recognised for its bridge engineering because of several world-renowned bridge projects that have had significant international impact. China's bridges account for more than half of the world's top-ten bridges under each category.

The awakened giant built an unprecedented record of airports in the world.

Chinese Civil Aviation Administration (CAAC) data shows that China had 241 certified transport airports at the end of 2020. At the end of 2020, China had fifty-eight more airports than it did just eight years earlier, in 2012. Approximately seven new airports are opened each year because of this.

The pace isn't slowing down. As a matter of fact, it is increasing. The Chinese government plans to have 400 airports for civil aviation by the end of 2035, an increase of 150 from 2020.

What awakened the sleeping giant in me?

"Thoughts are seeds for action."
James Cheng

The said statement impacted my life and awakened the sleeping giant in me."
Nelson Cheng

I was an introverted, unmotivated procrastinator and missed many opportunities in the early stage of life until I read this statement written by my brother James Cheng in his Bible: 'Thoughts are seeds for action.'

"**Thoughts are seeds for action.**"
James Cheng

This statement was totally awakening for me, and it has completely transformed my life ever since. The statement has been etched on the tablet of my heart ever since. The statement has become my credo of life, and it motivates me to put it into practice every time I come up with new thoughts or ideas.

This practice ultimately led me to become a leading inventor in Singapore with more than twenty-five filed patents and more than five hundred chemical products invented, one of Singapore's Top Entrepreneurs, the first and only Singaporean to win the World Packaging Organisation President Gold Award for sustainable packaging, a prolific author of books on anti-corrosion, and a co-author of more than 140 scientific journals.

In each of us lies a sleeping giant that must be awakened. It is my belief that we all possess one. It is up to each of us to tap the talents, gifts, and geniuses God has bestowed on us. Perhaps you are talented at selling or innovating. My belief is that our Creator does not play favourites, that we were all created uniquely, with equal opportunities to live a full and fulfilling life.

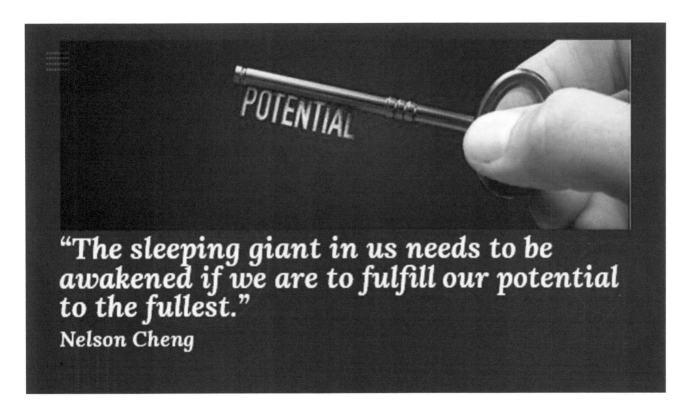

"The sleeping giant in us needs to be awakened if we are to fulfill our potential to the fullest."
Nelson Cheng

"If your mind is awakened, you will never stop pursuing dreaming."
Nelson Cheng

It is important to remember that awakening is not about changing who you are but about letting go of who you are not.
—Nelson Cheng

"Being awakened to the fact that there is a creator of this universe is one of the greatest awakenings in our lives."
Nelson Cheng

"By realizing just how precious each moment, each mental process, an each breath is, you can experience an awakening in your life."
Nelson Cheng

32
CHAPTER

Reflection on Persistence

There is one consistent characteristic of successful individuals around the world, regardless of their industry or culture, and that is their ability to persevere.

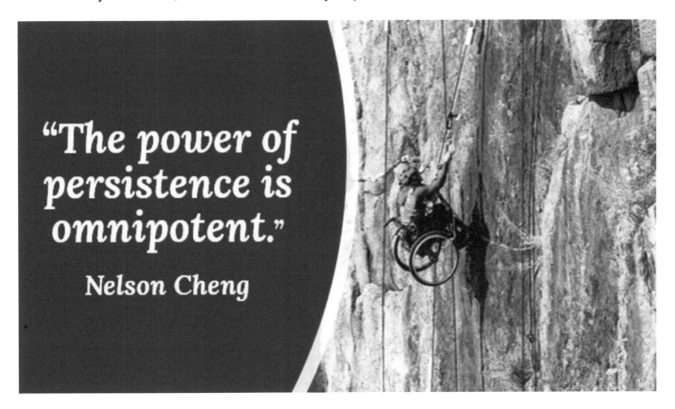

"The power of persistence is omnipotent."

Nelson Cheng

"The more persistence you demonstrate, the more you will succeed."
Nelson Cheng

Thomas Edison tried 999 times to perfect the light bulb but failed. He was asked, 'Are you going to have 1,000 failures?' to which he replied, 'I didn't fail—I just found another way not to invent the electric light bulb.'

As he perceived his previous experiences, he decided not to view them as failures.

Who better to represent Kentucky Fried Chicken than Colonel Sanders? He retired from the military with nothing but a recipe for chicken from his mother. How did he respond? Taking out his old sports wagon, he drove to restaurant after restaurant. It took him 1,007 times to receive his first yes before he finally succeeded in selling the chicken recipe. Kentucky Fried Chicken was made possible by that one yes.

Have the ability to stand up and make a change when everyone else is sitting down. Leaders like Abraham Lincoln, Martin Luther King Jr., Colonel Sanders, and Steve Jobs, just to name a few, have persevered beyond the norm.

Consider Abraham Lincoln. At the age of twenty-one, he failed in business. At the age of twenty-two, he lost a legislative race, failed again in business at the age of twenty-four, lost a congressional race at thirty-four and thirty-six, lost a senatorial race at forty-five, failed to become vice president at forty-seven, lost a senatorial race at forty-nine, and finally was elected president at fifty-two.

Without his persistence through those previous failures, what would our United States of America look like today?

"Your ability will be maximized by persistence."
Nelson Cheng

One word that describes entrepreneurs who succeed in business ownership is 'persistent'. Perseverance is key if you want to sustain your business through the challenges of entrepreneurship and ultimately reap the rewards of a successful business. There are many ups and downs to entrepreneurship. When you are starting a business, you sometimes feel that there are more downs than ups. For your business to succeed, you must maintain an optimistic and tough mindset throughout the hardships.

How do you develop persistence?

Clarify your reasons for wanting to do this

You will stay motivated through challenging times by identifying the deep purpose behind your goal. The best way to accomplish this goal is to write down what it means to you in detail.

Create a map of the possibilities

Determine how you can reach your goal using different means and methods. Getting the desired result can be achieved in several ways, I am sure we can all agree. Whatever the outcome, there are multiple routes to get there. The more ways you map out to reach your goal, the easier it will be to adjust if one strategy fails.

Get started

There can be no creation without measurable action. Don't be afraid to start and adjust as you go. The journey of an individual is often halted along the way. Failure doesn't define them or mean they'll never succeed just because they failed once. It simply means that, as Thomas Edison believed, they have found one more way to make it not work. As a result, they are one step closer to achieving their goal.

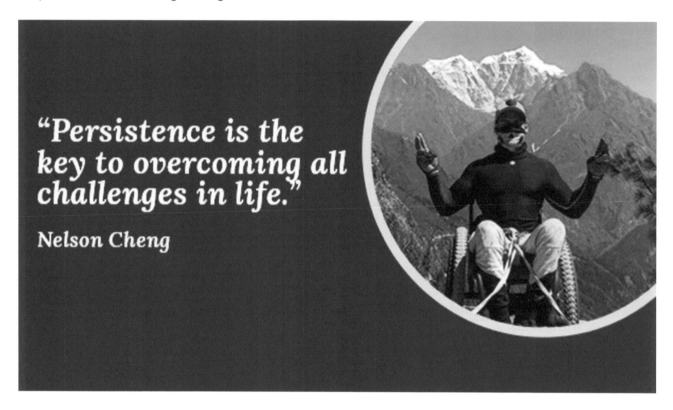

"Persistence is the key to overcoming all challenges in life."

Nelson Cheng

A person's persistence is defined as the ability to persist in doing something regardless of weaknesses, opposition, or difficulty.

33
CHAPTER

Reflection on Knowing Yourself

There is no such thing as being lost if you wander along many paths and dabble in many interests—but it is time to take an introspective look at yourself after roaming along many paths. This chapter covers how to stay strong in the long run by identifying your strengths and interests through knowing yourself.

You should know yourself well to make the best choices for yourself in life. It is important to know yourself before you know anyone else. Staying true to yourself throughout your life is important.

It's not just about knowing your favourite colour or food that you know who you are.

The key to knowing yourself is to ask yourself all the deep and intricate questions about who you are and how you think.

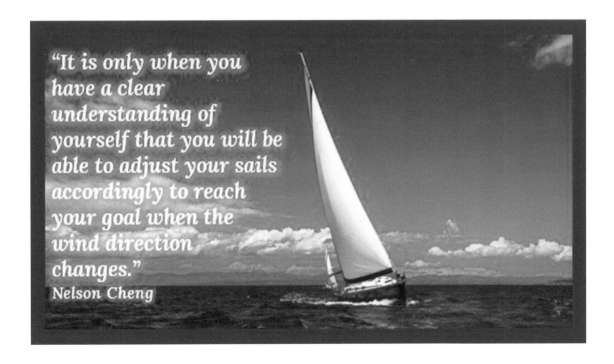

"It is only when you have a clear understanding of yourself that you will be able to adjust your sails accordingly to reach your goal when the wind direction changes."
Nelson Cheng

What knowing yourself entails

Knowing yourself is the experience of your own personality or individuality. It is about how you consciously understand your character, feelings, desires, strengths, and weaknesses.

One of the most important journeys of life is the journey of knowing yourself.

Life is a journey of self-discovery.

Self-formation is a continuous process based on the choices we make.

It is beneficial to an individual's development and well-being to have accurate self-awareness.

Since all our thoughts and emotions are so intricate, some argue that you can never truly know yourself. Although we may not be able to truly know ourselves inside out, we shouldn't let that stop us from striving for self-discovery. Every day, you'll learn more and more about yourself through introspection, journaling, talking to others, and reading inspirational quotes like these.

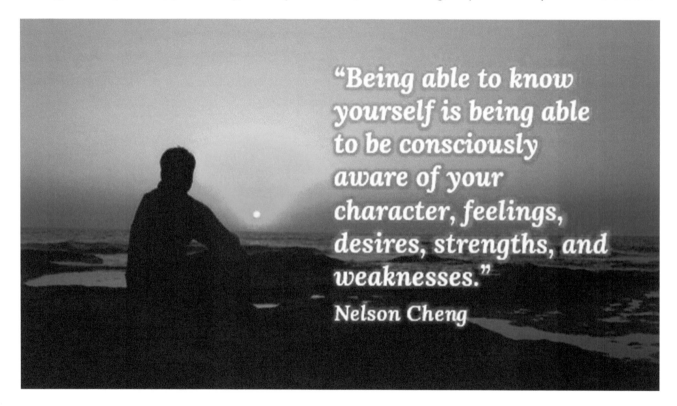

"Being able to know yourself is being able to be consciously aware of your character, feelings, desires, strengths, and weaknesses."
Nelson Cheng

How to know yourself

Give a brief description of yourself. Answering it can be a simple task: your name, your gender, your age, your height, your nationality, your interests, your likes and dislikes, your strengths and weaknesses, your hobbies, and your aspirations. Are you really who you say you are? What makes you, really, or is there more to it?

The first step to knowing ourselves is to love ourselves because it gives us a non-instrumental reason to do so, whereas self-respect demands that we do so.

It is important to identify your values and strengths to gain a deeper understanding of yourself. It's easy to identify your values and strengths when you feel strongly about certain things and excel in activities that make you feel good. You can gain a greater sense of self-awareness by reflecting on your past thoughts and actions, as well as observing your current behaviour. Considering these notions introspectively, and reflecting on them will also help you decide if they are true.

Having family and friends help you identify your strengths can also be helpful. A variety of in-depth personality or strength-profiling tests are available on the internet for free, including the DISC personality traits test. Nevertheless, such assessments should always be taken with a grain of salt.

'Those are the characteristics that define me as a human being.' You would write those things on a piece of paper if you were an object to purchase. Your identification card contains some of these things so that people know who you are and what you look like. Those are the things you say to be recognised more easily/faster by someone. However, that is not who you are. It's part of who you are.

The importance of knowing yourself

Being in a loving and respectful relationship with ourselves involves carefully pursuing a project of self-discovery for its own sake. The pursuit of self-knowledge may be a means of improving one's moral self-esteem and feeling satisfied with, while the absence of self-knowledge may lead to feelings of frustration and viciousness.

Your priority on the road to success is to know yourself.

When you don't know who you are or what you want, how can you realistically set goals, go about life, and have successful relationships? There is no way to do that.

Confusion and wasted time will result when you don't know yourself.

The importance of knowing oneself is often underestimated. We often react to events and just get by instead of making conscious choices based on who we are and what we want.

In the absence of a clear vision, it is difficult to set goals, motivate ourselves, and determine the best course of action. We must establish our identity before we can do any of these things. By knowing and understanding yourself better, you can make better decisions, set and achieve appropriate goals, and live a more fulfilling life.

"It is important to identify your values and strengths to gain a deeper understanding of yourself." Nelson Cheng

"Being in a loving and respectful relationship with ourselves involves carefully pursuing a project of self-discovery for its own sake." Nelson Cheng

"By knowing and understanding yourself better, you can make better decisions, set, and achieve appropriate goals, and live a more fulfilling life."

Nelson Cheng

It is extremely important to know yourself to make friends and understand your communication style. Knowing more about your thoughts, values, ideas, and personality helps you better plan your future.

Spend some time alone to understand yourself and then accept yourself to love yourself.

34

CHAPTER

Reflection on Ageing

"Aging is inevitable, hence preparation to extend our functional years is absolutely essential"
Nelson Cheng

Definition of ageing

Biologically, ageing is caused by the accumulation of molecular and cellular damage over time. As a result, physical and mental capacities gradually decrease, disease risks increase, and ultimately death occurs.

How does ageing affect humans?

Early adulthood marks the beginning of a gradual, continuous process of natural change. Early middle age is a time when many bodily functions begin to decline gradually. There is no specific age at which people become old or elderly. Age sixty-five has traditionally been considered the beginning of old age.

How does the ageing process work?

A person's bones tend to shrink as they age, weakening them and making them more susceptible to fractures. Even your height might decrease. Your coordination, stability, and balance can be affected when your muscles lose strength, endurance, and flexibility.

What are the signs of ageing?

- wrinkles and fine lines; the most noticeable and often most concerning signs of ageing are fine lines, crow's feet, and wrinkles.
- a dull complexion
- uneven tone to the skin
- skin that is dry
- the appearance of blotchiness and age spots
- a rough texture to the skin
- pores that are visible

In what ways does ageing affect us?

Several dynamic biological, physiological, environmental, psychological, behavioural, and social processes change as we age.

When does ageing begin?

The process of ageing is an inevitable part of life. Ageing begins at early middle age, which is a time when many bodily functions begin to decline gradually. Most of us start thinking about ageing in the later part of life when we start to see white hair on our heads and contour lines on our faces.

The misconception of ageing

It is common to think of life as a hump: we start as infants, grow into teens, and then mature into adults. It's all downhill from there. From improved public health to better transportation and better digital services, human development and technology have advanced to the point where our later years don't have to decline after a certain age.

Changing this orthodox mindset is necessary if we want to live a meaningful and fruitful senior life. Our senior years should therefore be planned if we want to live a meaningful and fruitful life or successful ageing process.

What are the problems of having rapidly ageing populations?

All developed countries are experiencing a rapidly ageing population. By 2050, nearly every country will have a larger share of the population aged sixty and over. Economic growth may be slowed by an ageing population because it tends to reduce labour force participation and savings rates.

Population ageing is posing social and economic challenges to industrialised, developed countries because of the shrinking share of young people. Working-aged people pay more to support the elderly, and public budgets strain under the burden of higher health and retirement costs for the elderly. Ageing populations and slow labour force growth affect economies in many ways.

It is becoming increasingly important to define successful ageing in terms of its quality. Keeping healthy and functioning for as long as possible is the focus of successful ageing.

Main issues of the ageing population

There is an unprecedented set of challenges arising as populations around the world age: shifting disease burdens, increased health-care expenditures, labour shortages, dissaving, and concerns about old-age income security.

Ageing program for successful ageing

As the population ages, it is necessary to implement an ageing program that is effective and efficient. In several countries such as Singapore, which has one of the fastest ageing populations in the world, and Japan, which has a 25 per cent elderly population, a successful ageing program has been successfully implemented.

Japan's and Singapore's governments have already seen positive results from innovative retirement income and care programs.

Singapore's successful ageing program

Singapore has prepared for population ageing at the national level. To coordinate government policies and programs related to population ageing, a Ministerial Committee on Ageing was established. Singapore's Action Plan for Successful Ageing was launched in 2015 as the nation's blueprint for ageing well.

With a life expectancy of around eighty-three years, Singapore is one of the world's fastest-ageing societies. To increase society's human capital potential as well as to promote personal development and social integration, its government has invested heavily in life-long learning initiatives.

Skills Future program

Every Singaporean aged twenty-five and above may attend approved skills-based courses with an opening credit of $500 through Skills Future, a national program launched in 2014. The government will periodically top up this credit so that it does not expire. As part of Skills Future, students and professionals can also participate in work-study programs to strengthen industry-academia interactions.

Lifelong learning program

Graduates of Singaporean universities are also supported in their pursuit of lifelong learning. During their matriculation year, alumni of the National University of Singapore can take selected industry-relevant courses for up to twenty years; the Singapore University of Social Sciences also offers alumni credits to offset fees for courses related to emerging skills.

Social risk pooling program

Other mechanisms are used in Singapore such as social risk pooling. The risk of outliving retirement resources and catastrophic health shocks is one of the most difficult risks to hedge for individuals. It may therefore accentuate income and wealth inequalities in society if old-age consumption is financed solely by individual efforts.

To address this need, CPF LIFE provides coverage for the retirement income needs of Singaporeans. During old age, the policyholder receives a monthly payout through compulsory contributions to the CPF account.

Medical program

MediShield Life, another scheme, covers Singaporeans' hospitalisation expenses for life. The plan covers large hospital expenses and some costly outpatient treatments, including dialysis and chemotherapy, and is funded through mandatory yearly premiums.

There is a need for our society to create an environment in which seniors are visible in society. Our community is a place where everyone is valued as a member, regardless of their age.

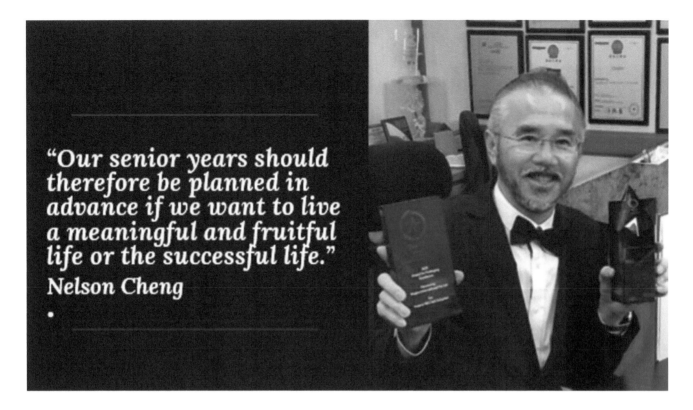

"Our senior years should therefore be planned in advance if we want to live a meaningful and fruitful life or the successful life."
Nelson Cheng

What is successful ageing?

Rather than only providing support to elderly people with chronic conditions, a forward-looking policy would aim to promote successful ageing from middle age onwards.

In biomedical theories, successful ageing is defined largely as maximising life expectancy while minimising physical and mental decline. The primary focus is on avoiding chronic disease and reducing risk factors for disease; good health; and independent physical, cognitive, and performance functions.

Hence, successful ageing emphasises how to extend functional years as we age.

From a biomedical perspective, the concept has evolved into a more comprehensive understanding of social and psychological adaptation in later life.

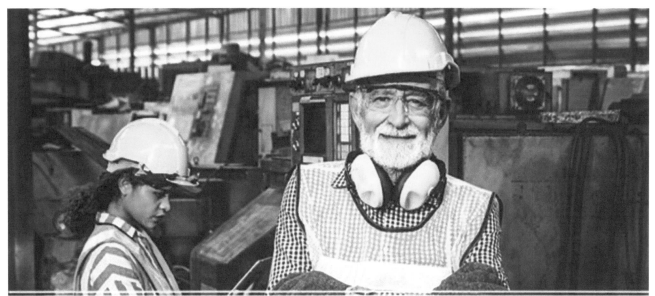

"Keeping healthy and functioning for as long as possible is the focus of successful aging." Nelson Cheng

Being active and engaged and continuing to learn are all important things seniors need to stay connected with their families and to stay informed about world events.

Many seniors decide to spend some of their golden years travelling to places they couldn't visit earlier in life. Some take time to travel to the extreme and end up breaking records in the process.

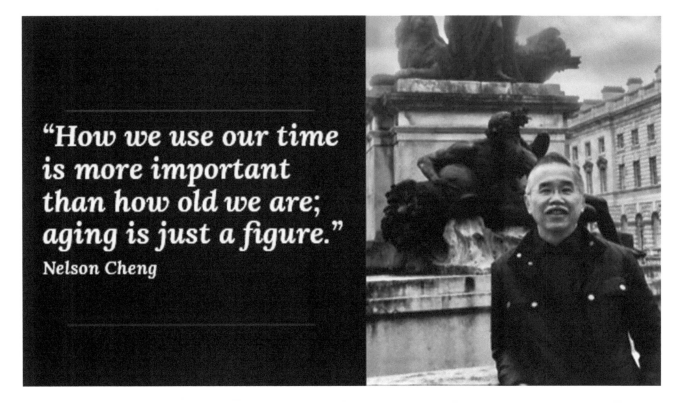

"How we use our time is more important than how old we are; aging is just a figure."
Nelson Cheng

35

CHAPTER

Reflection on the Two Essential Words in Life: 'Why' and 'How'

To learn and understand the world around me, asking why is a critical part of my learning process that leads to many of my inventions. I didn't realise until several years ago that many people don't use the same approach.

There appears to be a lack of interest in the reasoning behind the subject matter among so few people. When people ask questions, why do they tend to focus on what, where, when, and how? There is perhaps a certain personality type that makes us ask these kinds of 'big picture' and broader discovery questions. There is also a possibility that more people will consider asking these types of questions, but they are in a hurry and want to get to the details as soon as possible.

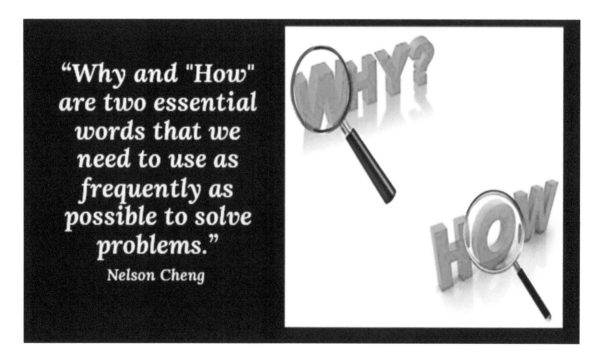

"Why and "How" are two essential words that we need to use as frequently as possible to solve problems."

Nelson Cheng

Analysing statements to find their reasons

Is there a reason to ask why? It is simple to answer that why questions are useful and provide reasons. With my experience in product development and solving complex technical problems, I have found that asking why I'm doing things builds understanding before I dive into the details.

By connecting the details in a broader context, they can be more easily understood and remembered. Hence, our perception of importance is shaped by the context of what we learn.

Ask yourself why you are making a decision next time you are making one. Think of how you can engage a client or customer at a higher level, where solutions to chronic problems or discovering new opportunities are more easily discovered. What is the reason for their need for assistance? Increase engagement and accelerate business success by focusing on that first and foremost. Whenever you lose sight of why, bring your actions back to the central goal. It's important to keep the reasons for doing something in mind before getting started.

The power of why comes with great responsibility! It can interfere with the ability of some people to focus and accomplish tasks if they are asked too many why questions as we all have different communication styles. Understand why you're doing what you're doing and when to ask. By doing this, not only will more effective conversations and exchanges be driven but time and energy may also be saved.

Why do we ask the question why?

Asking this recursively leads to a deeper understanding of the issue. This is the why of a problem solver. Many times, these two factors are intertwined or misinterpreted. There are times when the response to a question of justification is so compelling that it can lead to a change of heart.

What is the purpose of asking why?

It is important to question yourself if you want to change your life. Asking why can help us to understand where we want to go and how we want to grow. Why can have a profound impact on the way we live and can reshape the way we live as a society. As a result, we can bring about the change we want to see in the world.

"Why question can have a profound impact on the way we live and can reshape the way we live as a society."
Nelson Cheng

asking the
WHY QUESTION

What is the importance of asking why during conversation or discussion?

During a conversation or discussion, if you do not understand the purpose or rationale behind a particular topic, ask why.

Make sure you understand the conversation rather than simply continuing to talk.

Your character will be reflected in your ability to be fully present in every conversation. To gain a better understanding, ask questions. It is sometimes appropriate and right to ask the same question to another person. When gaining a deeper understanding, it may be more beneficial to ask a different question.

We are often encouraged to express our opinions and ask questions to demonstrate that we care. When you ask why, you gain answers and understanding, and you may display interest in the conversation or discussion.

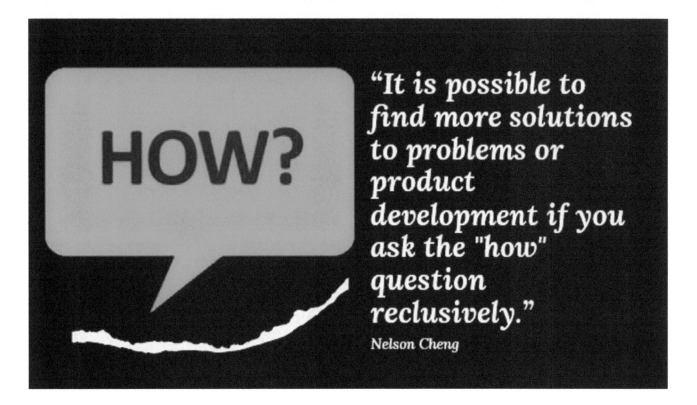

How does a how question work?

Both how and why are interrogative words, but they answer different questions. The word 'how' answers questions such as 'By what method?' 'To what extent?' 'Under what conditions?' and so on. Why answers questions such as 'For what purpose?'

What are some reasons to ask why and how questions?

Asking how leads to new discoveries. It's common to discover something new when you ask questions, whether they're related to something within the company.

Things are put together by you when you start to ask the how question.

Things seem to stick in your mind when you discover a new thing after asking the how question.

Issues are resolved by you when you ask the how question.

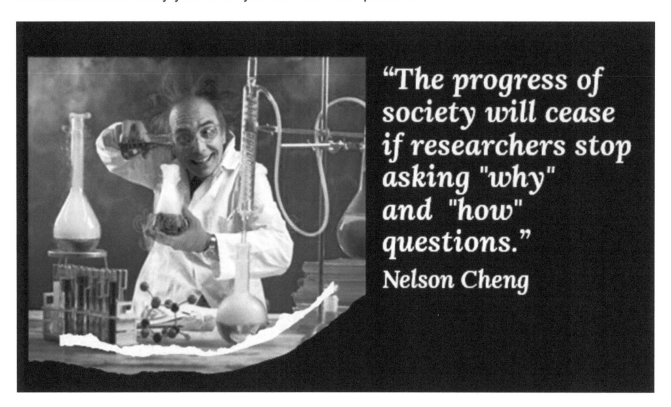

"The progress of society will cease if researchers stop asking "why" and "how" questions."
Nelson Cheng

Let's imagine a world where children no longer ask why and how. In what state will the world be in the future?

How will their societies fare?

How will their intellectual development be affected?

How will their standard of living be affected?

Take a moment to reflect on the questions above.

36

CHAPTER

Reflection on Gratitude

There is scientific evidence that gratitude increases happiness and fulfilment. When you are grateful, you focus on what you have instead of what you lack.

Appreciation and kindness are reciprocated when it is shown. Many of us are not used to practicing gratitude, even though the concept seems simple. It's not a character flaw; it's because society doesn't teach us to be grateful.

We are constantly told by marketing campaigns and advertising campaigns that we need more, and we are always told at work and school to be better. Even though this isn't necessarily a bad thing, it is incredibly powerful to take the time to be grateful for what you already have.

By practicing gratitude, people can boost their happiness, enjoy good experiences, improve their health, cope with adversity more effectively, and build strong relationships.

"It is important to remember that the highest expression of appreciation is to live by the words we use."
Nelson Cheng

How should we define gratitude?

The emotion of gratitude involves being grateful and appreciative and is associated with several mental and physical health benefits. An experience of gratitude involves feeling grateful for something or someone in your life and responding with kindness, warmth, and other forms of generosity.

What is the importance of gratitude?

"Being grateful; thankful, showing appreciation for and returning kindness is one of the gratitude's characteristics."
Nelson Cheng

Positive psychology research consistently shows that gratitude leads to greater happiness. Positive emotions, good experiences, improved health, coping with adversity, and strong relationships can all be attributed to gratitude.

In his essay 'Why Gratitude Is Good', Robert Emmons, perhaps the world's leading scientist on gratitude, describes gratitude's two key components. 'First of all,' he writes, 'it affirms goodness.' The world is full of good things, gifts, and benefits. Second, he explains that there are sources of goodness outside of ourselves that we should be grateful for. 'There are many people, or even higher powers if you are a spiritual person, who have given us gifts, big and small, that have helped us achieve our goals.'

Gratitude has a strong social dimension, according to Emmons and others. Emmons describes it as a relationship-strengthening emotion since it makes us realise how we have been supported and validated by others.

According to the sociologist Georg Simmel, gratitude is the moral memory of mankind since it encourages us to appreciate and repay gifts (or pay them forward). As a result, gratitude may have evolved through strengthened bonds between members of the same species that helped each other.

What are the characteristics of gratitude?

In fact, many of the characteristics of gratitude are pro-social: grateful people trust other people, help them, have empathy for them, forgive others, and do not hold grudges.

The quality of being thankful—readiness to show appreciation for and to return kindness—is another characteristic of gratitude. It's always important to reflect on all the blessings we have when cultivating an attitude of gratitude.

To be content in life, one must develop an attitude of gratitude.

It is important to remember that the highest expression of appreciation is to live by the words we use. Gratitude is essential to being content in life.
—Nelson Cheng

Gratitude can be cultivated only if we acknowledge that our success was due to the contribution of our family members, friends, and colleagues.

Only through acknowledging the contributions of family, friends, and colleagues can we cultivate gratitude.

"To be content in life, one must develop an attitude of gratitude."
Nelson Cheng

An Approach to Gratitude

Whenever you wake up each morning, contemplate the fact that you are alive and kicking. You can remain hopeful in all challenges if you contemplate the said fact. You can start developing a habit of gratitude each day by contemplating gratitude in the morning.

Practicing gratefulness regularly is a really easy way to enhance your own life and the lives of those around you. Gratefulness brings happiness and a deep knowing that life is beautiful.

How to practice gratitude

It is common to see our minds and bodies as one. The way we perceive ourselves is often influenced by our racial, linguistic, religious, national, educational, financial, and physical characteristics.

Gratitude doesn't come naturally to most of us, so we must practice it regularly to experience its benefits.

You must practice gratitude and work at it if you want to feel gratitude. As if you left the garden unattended, the weeds would take over. If you just let yourself go, if you just let your life be, then you won't have any gratitude. It takes work to be grateful, so it's a good thing to practice.

You should acknowledge your blessings every day, expressing gratitude for being alive, having children, and having a job. It takes effort to practice gratitude.

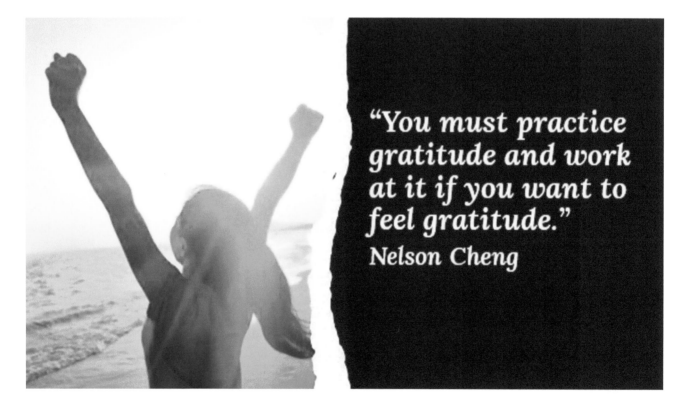

"You must practice gratitude and work at it if you want to feel gratitude."
Nelson Cheng

Search for gratitude in your challenges

Being thankful during negative or difficult situations is just as important as being thankful during positive times. In fact, it is usually times like this that can help us identify the positives in our life that we are most thankful for. Think back to past experiences that you have overcome and how it has strengthened you into the person you are today.

When you face challenges, look for gratitude.

Notes of gratitude should be written.

Gratitude can be expressed in a simple and effective way by sending thank-you notes. You and the recipient both benefit from them. In a study published in June 2018 in Psychological Science, it was revealed that the recipients of thank-you notes were more likely to feel not just happy but also 'ecstatic' after receiving the note. Zero awkwardness. Despite feeling strange, don't let that stop you from writing a thank-you note! There's a good chance you'll make someone's day. Employees' morale and productivity can be greatly enhanced by thank-you notes, emails, or announcements at work. For example, Employment Hero has integrated thank-you notes into its HR system, making it easy for employees to express their gratitude to one another.

37
CHAPTER

Reflection on Fears

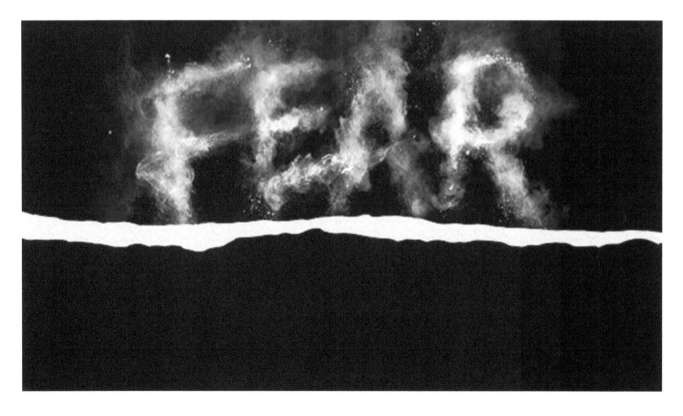

What is fear?

Fear is an unpleasant, often strong emotion that is induced by the anticipation or awareness of danger. Humans are prone to fear because it is a natural, powerful, and primitive emotion. Both a universal biochemical response and a high level of individual emotional response are involved. Whether it is physical or psychological danger, fear alerts us to its presence.

There are times when fear is triggered by real threats as well as times when it is triggered by imagined threats. Post-traumatic stress disorder (PTSD), social anxiety disorder, panic disorder, and phobias can also cause fear.

Fear is composed of two primary reactions to some type of perceived threat: reactions based on biochemical nature and a response based on emotion.

Reactions of biochemical nature

As a survival mechanism, fear is a natural emotion. The body responds in a specific way when confronted with a perceived threat. Fear causes us to sweat, increase our heart rate, and release high adrenaline levels, making us extremely alert.

As part of this physical response, your body prepares to enter combat or flee. Evolution likely led to this biochemical reaction. Our survival depends on this automatic response.

A response based on emotion

In contrast, fear has a highly personalised emotional response. Observing scary movies, for example, can make you feel fear since fear is a chemical reaction in our brains that also occurs with happiness and excitement.

There are those who thrive on adrenaline-inducing situations like extreme sports and other fear-inducing thrills. Fear-inducing situations are avoided at all costs by others with a negative reaction.

Regardless of the physical reaction, the experience of fear may be perceived positively or negatively depending on the person.

A list of fear-related symptoms

Emotional and physical symptoms are often associated with fear. The signs and symptoms of fear may differ from person to person, but the following are some of the most common:

- excessive sweating
- a trembling sensation
- an irregular heartbeat
- an upset stomach
- chest pain
- chills
- dryness in the mouth
- nausea
- shortness of breath

The psychological symptoms of fear may include feeling overwhelmed, upset, out of control, or as if death is imminent.

How to deal with fear?

An important human emotion, fear can help protect you from danger and prepare you for action, but it can also cause long-term anxiety. By learning how to cope with your fear and prevent anxiety from taking hold, you can better cope with these feelings.

You can also take steps to cope with fear daily. Managing fear physically, emotionally, and behaviourally involves such strategies. You can take the following actions:

Seek social support

It is possible to manage your feelings of fear by surrounding yourself with supportive people.

Put mindfulness into practice

Mindfulness can help you manage negative emotions and replace them with more helpful ones, even though you cannot always prevent certain emotions.

Relax your muscles through progressive muscle relaxation

Deep breathing and visualisation.

Maintain a healthy lifestyle

Get enough sleep every night, eat well, and exercise regularly.

How can you overcome your fears?

It will hold us back and cause more problems if we avoid everything that makes us anxious. We increase our fears in our minds by avoiding things we fear. We can become stronger by facing our fears.

To face fears, we must expose ourselves to fear. As you expose yourself to feared situations, you become less anxious as you go into them more slowly and repeatedly. There is no danger in exposing yourself to fear, and it won't worsen it. You will naturally become less anxious after a while.

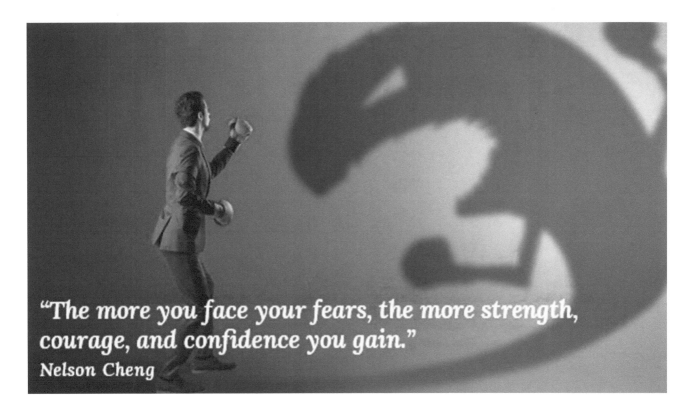

"The more you face your fears, the more strength, courage, and confidence you gain."
Nelson Cheng

What you can do to stop living in fear

Fear can only be overcome by facing it. The only thing that prevents us from moving forward is avoiding our fears—it makes us anxious. Do only what feels safe for you, and be gentle with yourself.

Whenever you feel fearful, take a break and notice something pleasant or comforting. If it feels safe later, you can explore your fear again, taking breaks when necessary.

Therapy can be invaluable if you find it difficult to overcome chronic fears or anxiety on your own. It is especially important to work with a therapist if you have experienced trauma to create a safe environment where you can confront your fears and reconstruct your memories.

If you are fearful, you can use the tips listed below to help you cope.

- Analyse the cause of your anxiety.
- Don't let fear get in the way of your goals.
- It's time to stop making excuses.
- Put an end to your 'should' and turn them into 'musts'.
- Ask what you are fearful about.
- Understand that pain provides valuable insight.
- Maintain a healthy lifestyle.
- Think abundance instead of scarcity.

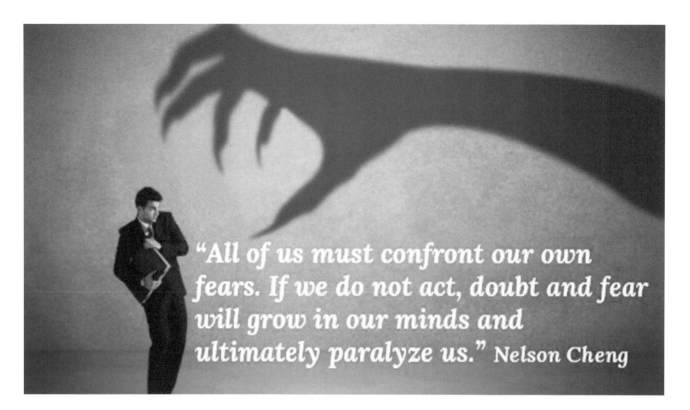

"All of us must confront our own fears. If we do not act, doubt and fear will grow in our minds and ultimately paralyze us." Nelson Cheng

38
CHAPTER

Reflection on Forgiveness

Forgiveness is generally defined as a conscious, deliberate decision to release feelings of resentment or vengeance towards a person or group who has harmed you, regardless of whether they deserve your forgiveness.

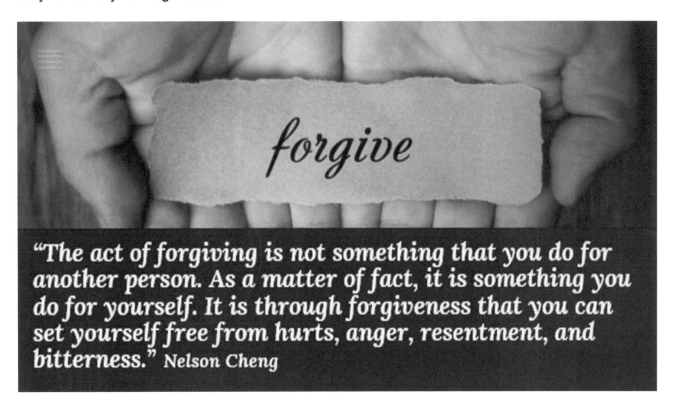

forgive

"The act of forgiving is not something that you do for another person. As a matter of fact, it is something you do for yourself. It is through forgiveness that you can set yourself free from hurts, anger, resentment, and bitterness." Nelson Cheng

In the face of hurt, you can hold on to anger, resentment, and thoughts of revenge—or you can embrace forgiveness and move on with your life.

"By forgiving others, you can break the chains and shackles of grudges and bitterness."
Nelson Cheng

The consequences of unforgiveness

It is common for people to justify grudges by claiming that the offender has done nothing to deserve forgiveness, but holding on to those grudges stunts our progress.

As a result of spending time and energy thinking about the issue, people hold grudges because they are unsure of what would happen if they released it.

Unforgiveness is a hindrance to healing and deliverance, and it can open doors to demons if held for too long. Our prayers can also be hindered when we store our emotions within our hearts rather than releasing them.

"If you hold on to a grudge, you may think you are in control, but in reality, you are letting the offense control you."
Nelson Cheng

"The longer you hold onto unforgiveness, the more bitterness, offense, and hurt you will experience, ultimately you will be caged in the sphere of bitterness and rage."
Nelson Cheng

The benefits of forgiveness

Have you ever wanted to move on but had difficulty figuring out how to do so? The tendency to justify an uncomfortable emotion and hold on to the behaviour that follows is a tough one to resist. As a matter of fact, it's called payback. When feelings arise because you have been unfairly treated, what do you do? When we react negatively to this, we can become trapped in destructive patterns.

By forgiving an offender, healing can occur no matter where the offender is located or how he or she behaves. Forgiveness may mean different things to those who struggle with issues of abuse and injustice. Some people may be reluctant to forgive, fearing that the process will make them weaker and more vulnerable.

Studies have shown that people who forgive are more likely to have higher self-esteem, lower blood pressure, fewer stress-related health problems, better immune system function, and lower heart disease rates.

It is even possible to feel empathy, compassion, and understanding for the one who hurt you when you forgive. The act of forgiveness does not mean forgetting or excusing what happened to you, nor does it mean making up with the person who did it. When you forgive, you can move on with your life with a sense of peace.

In the end, forgiveness benefits you the most. With this small choice, you can experience God's peace, joy, and freedom in a way you never thought possible. By releasing unforgiveness, you are free from what had enslaved you.

There is power in forgiveness. Getting to a place where you can forgive people is not an easy journey, but it frees you, and that's why it's so powerful.

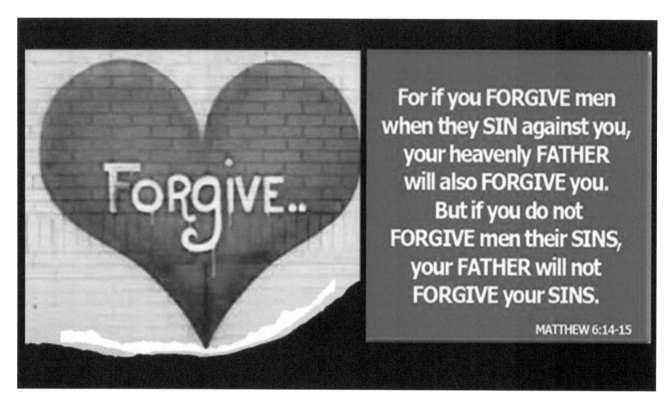

"In contrast to what others believe, forgiveness is more about healing yourself than healing another person. Grudges hurt, and bitterness is released through forgiveness."
Nelson Cheng

Forgiveness heals

To forgive is to let go of all anger, resentment, or other negative feelings and thoughts towards the person who has wronged you. There will be no easy path through this process. Depending on the individual, each step will differ.

While forgiveness does not change the past, it can change the perception of it, which will result in a change in how you process it, which will ultimately lead to a change in how you tell it. It's forgiveness that heals the body, refreshes the mind, and encourages the soul.

As you let go of the past hurts, you become free from its grip, which allows you to feel a sense of freedom within yourself. If you forgive, you are giving yourself one of the greatest gifts of all. Everybody should be forgiven.

We can express our love within our souls through forgiveness, and letting go of our hurts allows us to grow. The ability to forgive must be developed and maintained. A person who is incapable of forgiving is incapable of loving.
—Nelson Cheng

Accepting mistakes and forgiving (even if the other party did not ask for forgiveness) can help heal unseen wounds. Feelings of freedom and expansiveness are created as a result.

Ways to forgive and move on

Acknowledge the hurt

You are doing this for yourself, so remind yourself of that.

The journey to forgiveness is not easy; often, it's a road filled with resentment. If we keep on thinking that the one who has hurt us should apologise, we might be disappointed.

When it comes to forgiveness, there's always a shift, a realisation that you are unloading the burden of grudges off your heart, away from your soul. Forgiveness is about you.

Make peace with yourself by reconciling with others

We can become impatient with ourselves when we make bad choices that have bad effects. It is common for us to blame ourselves for being so rash, impulsive, and unwise. When it comes to forgiveness, forgiving ourselves is an important first step.

Sometimes, we make mistakes, make unwise choices, and even come up with the worst ideas. Making peace with yourself is just as important as making peace with your painful experiences.

Understanding instead of blaming

Not only can it be tempting to play the blame game, but it can also be debilitating. Holding on to grudges and resentments results from blaming others. Peace can be gained by understanding what we went through.

Identify support sources

There are times when all we want is someone to listen to us. We are more likely to forgive when we have a supportive network to encourage us to do so.

Kindness is more important than being right

Do you have a petty argument with your partner? Do you have a family member who makes snide remarks? It's best to just let it go and move on if you feel it's insignificant. Your healing process will be kicked off by this.

Kindness is more important than being right. There are times when it's the only thing that can bring you peace and improve your mental health.

39
CHAPTER

Reflection on Bitterness of Life

"The seeds of bitterness are small at first. It is easy for an offense to burrow its way into our hearts."
Nelson Cheng

How is bitterness developed

It is inevitable that there will be conflict in life, whether it is between friends or family members. Unresolved conflicts can lead to long-term grudges and hatred.

Someone plants the seed of bitterness in their heart because of being hurt. Whether it is intentional or unintentional is up to you. Even though someone didn't intend to hurt you, you were hurt. There are times when the hurt is only imagined. You have not been hurt, but somehow you feel you have been wronged by someone.

The seeds of bitterness are small at first. It is easy for an offence to burrow its way into our hearts. As we replay it in our minds, we create deep ruts that are difficult to overcome. Each sordid detail of our hurts is retold to any listener available. As a result, we enlist support, which pushes us deeper into our resentment. Whenever we hear the offending person's name, we cringe.

We perceive the offence as intentional and our offender as spiteful. In addition to the real or imagined reasons we dislike our villain, we look for other reasons. A new layer of bitterness is formed with every new piece of information.

Anger and resentment can seep into everything even if we think no one will notice. It's like trying to submerge a beach ball in the water. Despite all our efforts, it pops up with all its vitality and splashes everyone.

Bitter people are angry and unhappy because they cannot forget the bad things that have happened to them. Hostility and a refusal to deal with hurt are the soil of bitterness. It takes root in the heart and grows deeper when someone becomes bitter.

The world is full of people who haven't resolved old hurts. Their goal is to find fault with others, criticise things, and justify their feelings. Have you ever seen someone who is hypercritical? There is a tendency for them to be bitter people.

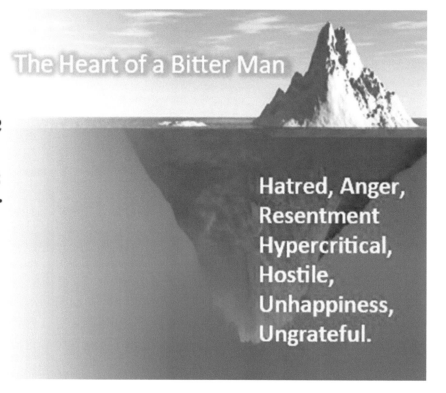

"The seeds of bitterness are small at first. It is easy for an offense to burrow its way into our hearts. As we replay it in our minds, we create deep ruts that are difficult to overcome."
Nelson Cheng

The Heart of a Bitter Man

Hatred, Anger, Resentment Hypercritical, Hostile, Unhappiness, Ungrateful.

What is the fruit of bitterness?

The bitterness that takes root in us produces fruit that wounds anyone who tastes it.

It is easy to conceal and camouflage bitterness underground. It is rare to find someone who admits to being bitter. Their response will be either to deny it or to disguise it. An individual who is bitter is hypersensitive, ungrateful, insincere, holds grudges, and has mood swings.

Since bitterness is just like an acid that destroys its container; it will affect you physically, emotionally, and spiritually. Bitterness in your heart makes God seem unreal to you. What's the reason? It is impossible for holiness and hatefulness to dwell together in the same heart. Hebrews 12:14 says, 'Make every effort to live in peace with everyone and to be holy; without holiness, no one will see the Lord.'

How to eradicate bitterness

Everyone has flaws. Letting go is the first step. Recognising that everyone has flaws and accepting that we all have faults is vital to letting go of your victim role. Most of the time, the wrong done to you reflects the offender rather than you. There is no purpose to it in your mind or your life, and how you've been hurt shouldn't define who you are.

You must confront the underlying causes of bitterness and resentment to overcome them. Many people who feel bitter or resentful leave their feelings unaddressed in their minds.

Consider the bitterness and resentment you're experiencing. Try to understand why you are feeling this way and when the feelings began to appear.

What did you find most upsetting about that situation? How were personal values offended or threatened? What makes those values important to you? Forgiveness begins with addressing that core issue.

Forgiveness is essential. Choosing to overcome bitterness and resentment is the key to overcoming them. Because of the pain, we often miss the fact that we have a choice in our response to some circumstances. A second requirement is that we be willing to do whatever it takes, including forgiving.

It is important to realise that few things on earth are guaranteed during your lifetime. Ageing process, suffering, and being hurt by people are just a few of the things you will experience. Considering the knowledge that we are bound to get hurt during our short time on earth will help us to mentally process the pain of getting hurt without becoming bitter or resentful. By forgiving, you will be able to move forward in the relationship without bitterness or resentment.

You must choose forgiveness from the bottom of your heart. Forgiveness is a conceptualised internal process. When a transgression has occurred, the individual decides to let go of the negative feelings associated with it.

It is spiritual and not psychological to forgive since forgiveness is a heart attitude, not a mental one. It is possible to forgive mentally before we can forgive from the heart.

When we say 'I forgive you', our hearts must be ready to forgive, followed by our minds. Our minds tend to replay the event on repeat in our heads when we forgive with our minds before we forgive with our hearts.

Make forgiveness a habit. As you practice forgiveness and take your thoughts captive, you become more capable of forgiving someone. Strengthening forgiveness is like strengthening a muscle.

There will be many people who will tell you to forgive but don't forget. There is no such thing as heart forgiveness—the attitude of forgiveness.

Forgiving and forgetting are not the same thing because a man is as he thinks in his heart. The more you dwell on the fact that someone has hurt you, the more bitterness and anger you're likely to experience.

There will be thoughts of the past, but we must live in the present, not in the past. Remember, you have forgiven the person and moved forward with your life when they captured your thoughts.

Get over grudges. Let go of grudges to overcome bitterness and resentment. Grudges are formed when anger cannot be expressed directly. The people who hold grudges have rigid personality structures. The field of psychology considers rigidity unhealthy.

It is healthy to be flexible, open, and fluid, especially since feelings change constantly. Strong egos are capable of handling disappointments, life's inevitable ups and downs, and daily disappointments.

Getting revenge is commonly motivated by rejection and abandonment. When we feel discarded or thrown away, it evokes a primitive feeling of rage, reminiscent of how we felt as babies when our mothers ignored or failed to respond to our needs.

If you 'just let it go', you will be left holding your intense rage with nowhere to release your aggressive impulses. To 'just let it go', a person needs to be unusually positive, optimistic, and easy-going.

You are the one who benefits in the end. Holding on to anger, hostility, aggression, and rage has been known to cause medical illnesses.

The negativism of bitterness

In most cases, holding on to bitterness will result in the loss of a relationship. The people who mean the most to us often evoke the greatest level of hurt and anger in us. It's not a small risk, but you might lose a significant relationship.

Holding on to bitterness can also cause physical and medical harm. Among them are heart disease, high blood pressure, headaches, digestive imbalances, insomnia, anxiety and depression, and skin problems like eczema and stroke.

It is temporary to gain revenge by acting out. After purging all your harmful anger and hate, you might feel euphoria. Many people, however, think of the guilt that follows hostile payback and worry about the consequences.

Bitterness and resentment will destroy you. Psychologists define bitterness as an attitude of widespread and intense anger and hostility, often accompanied by resentment and the desire to seek revenge.

Bitterness is keeping a record of wrong, where a person holds on to the transgression and mulls it over and over in his or her mind. A resentful person typically wants to or thinks about getting even with the transgressor. In a way, resentful people cannot stop thinking about the transgression against them.

In short, bitterness is a result of deep resentment and unforgiveness in your heart, and there lies the problem. You're experiencing unforgiveness.

Ironically, many people view bitterness, resentment, and unforgiveness as psychological problems. What many of us forget is we are spirit, mind, and body. Therefore, it is most helpful to look at bitterness, resentment, and unforgiveness as spiritual problems, not psychological problems.

Decide not to be bitter

Bitterness isn't something others do to you; it's something you choose. When you are wronged, you can either hold on to it and become bitter or let it go. The pain of being hurt by someone we care about is understandable.

To live a healthy life, you must forgive. Neither forgetting nor excusing the harm done nor even reconciling with the offender means forgetting. Inner peace brought by forgiveness can reduce anxiety, improve mental health, and lower blood pressure.

40
CHAPTER

Reflection on Contentment of Life

Instead of attempting to satisfying all our desires, we need to learn how to limit them to find contentment in life.

Having a sense of contentment is one of life's greatest joys. Contentment is a priceless gift that makes you happy. An individual who is content with who they are and what they have is simply happy, fulfilled, and satisfied with where they are in life.

Instead of appreciating God for what they have, many people worry about what they don't have.

A state of contentment is not synonymous with a state of complacency. Living out your purpose passionately gives you a sense of fulfilment. There is a difference between contentment and complacency. The moment you stop growing, you begin to die.

If you try to run another person's race in life, you will never win. Don't forget to celebrate the gifts and blessings of God upon others.

What is contentment?

As you reflect on all the things you are grateful for, you will feel a sense of contentment. Happiness and satisfaction are the results of contentment. A contented state of mind is not an exciting kind of happiness. Instead, it is a relaxed and peaceful state of mind.

Being content refers to being at ease with one's circumstances, spirit, soul, and body. A state of contentment, in colloquial terms, is the acceptance of one's situation and is a milder and more tentative form of happiness.

Contentment can also be defined as an ideal state of mind achieved through being happy with what one has instead of achieving one's larger goals.

The pursuit of contentment is a central theme in many philosophical or religious schools across diverse cultures, eras, and regions.

How to develop contentment

Realise that we will leave this world with nothingness

According to the Bible, 'But godliness with contentment is great gain. For we brought nothing into this world, and it is certain we can carry nothing out' (1 Tim. 6:6–7 [KJV]).

We must first acknowledge that we were born without bringing anything into this world, and we cannot carry anything out of it either. The said Bible verses are fundamentals in developing contentment.

Learn to be grateful

Contentment cannot be developed without gratitude—they are inseparable. Gratitude will make a person happy no matter what they have. Focus on what you have rather than what you lack. You will be more content in your life if you are grateful for what you have. Live a happy life and laugh more.

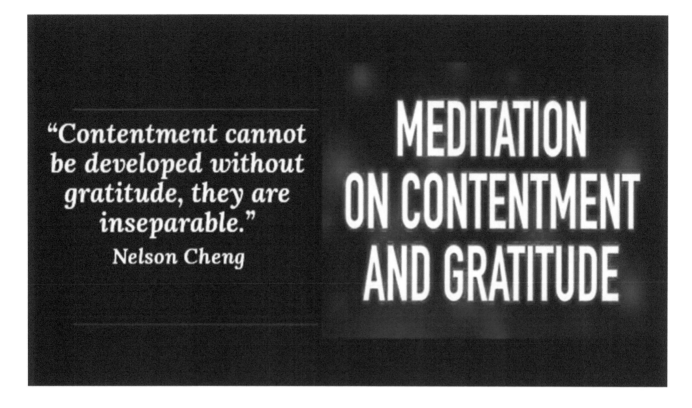

"Contentment cannot be developed without gratitude, they are inseparable."
Nelson Cheng

MEDITATION ON CONTENTMENT AND GRATITUDE

Limit our desires

My contentment has been found in limiting my desires rather than attempting to fulfil them.

Contentment can be achieved by letting go of the love of money and being content with what you have.

Learn to embrace minimalism

In addition to facilitating minimalism, contentment also reduces stress levels, improves outlooks, relaxes bodies, and enhances the quality of life.

In minimalism, there is an unmistakable sense of freedom: to be yourself, to enjoy yourself, and to live the life you were meant to live. Your sense of happiness and joy shouldn't come from material possessions.

Our consumeristic culture encourages discontent and material gratification, making it hard for us to learn to be content. Everyone's journey to becoming a minimalist will look different, so it is certainly a personal journey.

Embrace each moment as it comes

Don't wait for a day when your life will be less hectic or less stressful before enjoying joy. You may never see that day.

Consider savouring the small pleasures of everyday life instead. Do not dwell on the past or worry about the future but concentrate on the positives in the present moment.

You can improve your happiness by cultivating a grateful attitude, being optimistic, focusing on your purpose, and living in the present. Take steps today towards being a happier person, and incorporate these strategies into your daily life.

Embrace optimism

Become accustomed to seeing things from a positive perspective. It's important not to become unduly optimistic—after all, bad things can happen. There is no point in pretending otherwise. Despite the negatives, you don't have to let them dictate your outlook. It is almost always more important to remember what is right about you than what is wrong.

The process of changing your pessimistic thinking may take time if you are not an optimistic person by nature. Begin by recognising your negative thoughts. Once you have taken a step back, ask yourself these questions:

Does the situation really seem as bad as I imagine?

Could the situation be viewed in a different way?

Is there anything I can learn from this experience that I can apply in the future?

Take time to appreciate what you have

It is possible to be grateful for what you have but not appreciate what you have. Having an appreciation for what you have will help you succeed in life. Your special abilities and gifts are unique. Success begins with appreciating who you are.

The acquisition of any possession does not guarantee your happiness. One of the most important life lessons you can ever learn is that happiness depends entirely on your decision to be happy.

Identify your purpose

Growing a garden, caring for children, and honouring one's spirituality are all examples of fulfilling a goal or fulfilling a mission that makes people happier than those who don't.

Goals provide a sense of purpose, strengthen self-esteem, and bring people together. If the process of working towards your goal is meaningful to you, it doesn't matter what your goal is.

Aim to align your daily activities with your life's long-term meaning and purpose. The strongest meaning and purpose in life can be found in relationships, according to research studies. Develop meaningful relationships.

What do you love to do? Find out if you can find your purpose by asking yourself these questions:

Is there anything that excites and energises me?

What are my proudest accomplishments?

In what way do I want to be remembered by others?

Give back to others

The focus is taken off you when you help others. You will learn to be content when you begin helping others and sharing your time, money, and talents. Through practice, you will gain a deeper appreciation of what you own, who you are, and what you have to offer. As you learn to help people, you will soon realise how powerful and rich you truly are.

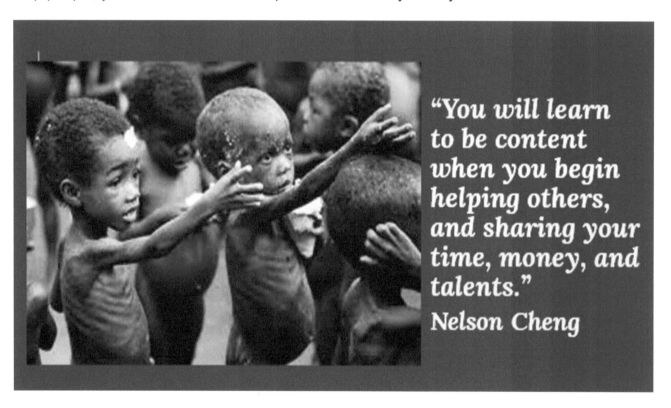

"You will learn to be content when you begin helping others, and sharing your time, money, and talents."
Nelson Cheng

Stop satisfying discontentment with new acquisitions

You won't find more joy in life by purchasing another new dress, shoe, car, or piece of furniture. We have been conditioned to believe that the best way to diffuse discontent is to purchase the outward object that seems to be causing it. The true cause of dissatisfaction is rarely determined. Refrain from succumbing to discontentment the next time you notice it surfacing in your life. Try to understand yourself and why you are dissatisfied without that item. The only way to achieve true contentment is to break this habit intentionally.

Make the most of your resources

Do not be satisfied with where you are or what you have, but with who you are and what you have. It is never too late to improve yourself, to learn, to grow, or to discover new things.

Keeping things simple

The idea is to be content with less, with a simpler and richer life, instead of always wanting more, acquiring more, possessing more, and never being satisfied.

Celebrate the achievements of others

Celebrating others' achievements, even those who seem more successful than you, requires cultivating the wonderful gift of contentment.

Work with what you've got

Discontentment paralyses you from using your talents and gifts because of its negative effects. You'll be surprised that your gifts and talents are exactly what your world needs to make a difference, no matter how small they seem.

Be more prayerful

It is through prayer that we can appreciate even the smallest things in life. When we pray, our pride is broken, and we are humbled. The habit of praying every day should become a part of your routine.

Evaluation of discontentment

The goal is to understand why you want more and to resolve the root cause of that desire. Being unsatisfied with what one has is at the root of wanting more. Being content is the key to living a fulfilled life.

Contented people seem to intuitively understand that their contentment is the sum of their life choices, and their lives are built on the following pillars: taking time to spend with family and friends, being grateful for what they have, keeping an optimistic attitude, having a purpose in life, and taking time to enjoy the moment.

How to be content

If you've been looking for contentment, the good news is that your choices, thoughts, and actions can influence your level of contentment. It's not as easy as flipping a switch, but you can turn up your contentment level. Here's how to get started on the path to creating a happier you.

"Make the most of what you have; otherwise, when one is not content with what one has, he is not likely to be contended with what one wants."

Nelson Cheng